AGONISE
WITH
HILLIE

FIRST DATE

PAVLOS

AGONISE
WITH
HILLIE

'HILLIE MARSHALL'S ANSWERS
TO PERSONAL PROBLEMS IN THE 90'S'

SUMMERSDALE

Summersdale Publishers
46 West Street
Chichester
West Sussex
PO19 1RP
United Kingdom

A CIP catalogue record for this book
is available from the British Library.

ISBN 1 873475 80 2

Typeset by Annabel Jackson.

Printed and bound in Great Britain
by Selwood Printing Ltd.

To
Paul, Anne, Lee, Angela, Keith, Julie,
Helen, Anita, Anthony, Marilyn, Melody,
Stewart, Alastair,
The 'Corfu Gang', John & Bitten

and not forgetting the two most important people in my life
Nicola and Jamie!

Contents

Introduction

This book is a compilation of the many problems I have received and answered as an Agony Aunt on the Internet, Television and Radio, in Magazines, from the members of Dinner Dates, family and friends. I hope that this collection gives a representative view of the many problems we all encounter in the '90's today, and that my answers to them may be of help to you all.

Foreword

By Peter Stringfellow

I first met Hillie Marshall over 20 years ago. I'd taken my wife Coral and our two children, Scot and Karen, to Tunisia for our first family holiday. Every evening we would all dress up for dinner which is something I thought everyone did on holiday. On our third evening, a very attractive lady came over to our table and said she would like to congratulate us for being such a wonderful family. Her name was Hillie and she was staying in the same hotel with her husband, Tony. Although our backgrounds were very different; Tony worked in the City and I owned Cinderella/Rockerfellas in Leeds, something clicked and we all became friends. We made arrangements to meet after the holiday, but as everyone knows, holiday friendships rarely come to fruition. It's all kissipoos, exchanging phone numbers and promises of I'll ring you, then everyone forgets when they get home.

This holiday friendship was different. When we got back to Leeds, I invited Tony and Hillie to the club and they then invited Coral and I to stay with them in London. They had a beautiful apartment overlooking Regents Park so whenever we came to London, Hillie would make us welcome. A new Hillie came forward in London, she wasn't only the glamorous wife and wonderful host, but a brilliant Cabaret singer. It wasn't until Coral and I went to watch her sing one night that I realised what a modest lady she was. Then one evening I saw another side to Hillie. She had lent me her Mini one day on the promise that I would return it in time for her to go to work in a show. It was typical of me to be 25 minutes late and suddenly wonderful Hillie revealed another side to her character, and let me know in no uncertain terms what she felt about my time keeping. She threw out a whole new vocabulary that left me shocked. She isn't a lady to bear a grudge so by the following day I was forgiven and the incident forgotten.

Over the years we kept in touch. She and Tony came to the opening of my Millionaire club in Manchester, and then later, Stringfellows in London. They eventually had two children, Nicola and Jamie and always seemed like the perfect happy-go-lucky family. Yet things are never what they seem. Cracks began to show in their marriage which echoed the cracks in my own marriage to Coral. Although Hillie was always protective and loyal to Tony, it was clear that things were not working out for them. One day I called Tony and was shocked to find out that they were no longer together. Hillie had made every effort in her marriage, she was always glamorous, fun, loving, and a great mother, but sometimes things disintegrate no matter how hard we try. I know this from my own marriage to Coral. We had 23 wonderful years together but eventually we had to part. I stayed friends with both Hillie and Tony and although we could often go months, sometimes years without seeing one another, we would always pick up where we left off.

One day Hillie called out of the blue to say that she had started a singles dining and social events club called *Dinner Dates*. Much to my shame, I was rather sceptical. I couldn't see Hillie now living alone with her children, as the go-getting business woman. I was wrong. She asked if one of her first evenings could be held at Stringfellows, so of course I was happy to help. Like a lot of people I had a rather negative image of what a singles evening would be like. I imagined these people were misfits, which was way off the mark. Hillie turned up with 16 lovely people and spent the evening going round the tables introducing people like they were all her long lost friends. She has a wonderful way with people, an openness that immediately puts people at their ease. That evening I saw another side to the independent, I-can-do-it-on-my-own, Hillie. She and Tony were still friends, yet she was now the single girl again, with a whole new career.

Within a year, Hillie's singles club was one of the most successful in London. She built it in the aftermath of her marriage break-up and while raising two children, so you can imagine what a dedicated and determined lady she is. Not only did she create and build a business, she also managed to write her own book.

Hillie Marshall's Guide to Successful Relationships was a huge success, but typical of Hillie, she forgot to tell me she was an author and Agony Aunt. It wasn't until she called to ask me to write a foreword for this book that yet another of her talents came to light. She's experienced a great deal over the years and always managed to come out of whatever situation smiling and determined. Lots of people run away from their problems, hoping that they will go away if only they could stop thinking about them. Hillie is the opposite. She is prepared to deal with life's problems and prepared to listen and help other people. I'm sure this book will be a great success. I'm also sure that some time in the near future, I'll get a call, informing me of the film that she's written and is about to star in. I've known Hillie long enough to know that she can make anything happen.

Peter Stringfellow (August 1996)

KIDS

'Why can't I stay up late?'
Problems Children have
with Parents

Q My Mum's such a cow. She never lets me go to bed when I want to, and now it's the holidays I'm only allowed to go to bed half an hour later at 10pm. All my friends are the same age as me (I'm a 12 year old boy) and can stay up much later, and my sister (who's 16) can go to bed whenever she wants to. It's not fair. Why can't *I* stay up late?
James, Chester

A *You are not allowed to stay up late because, contrary to your present belief, your Mum is not a 'cow'; she is a very caring parent who is anxious about your well being. It is a fact of life that boys of your age need much more sleep than a young adult of 16. At your age you will be going through puberty, and your body will be using so much energy for growth, that if you do not allow it enough rest you will get ill and not be able to function properly. Nothing much happens after 10pm (which is of interest to boys of your age) that can't be done before this hour, and television programmes will be for adult viewing only. If you go to bed late, you will wake up late (because you need the sleep) and miss out on the day. Mark my words, when you are an adult you will give anything for a few extra hours in bed!*

Q I am just 12 and I have a very developed body for my age. I am sure that I need a bra as I feel uncomfortable when I run or play games at school. My parents haven't said anything, and I am embarrassed to talk to them. I would like to go and buy a bra, but I don't get enough pocket money. Should I just ask for more pocket money or borrow from friends? I'm just too embarrassed to talk to my mother!
Tina, Durham

A Just remember that your mother was your age once, and I'm sure she probably experienced the same difficulties then, that you are having to cope with now. Only you know how uncomfortable your breasts are at present, and even if your parents have noticed how much your body has developed, they may think that like many girls today you don't want to wear a bra. Wearing a bra is just a normal necessity for a girl, so 'chin up', and have a chat with your mother. If you don't ask, she won't know, and you won't get!

Q My mother insists on giving me 'hand-me-down' clothes from cousins and friends' daughters, and I hate having to wear them. I'm 11 and I'm old enough to choose my own clothes and I feel embarrassed about what I wear now. What can I do about it?
Jennifer, Surrey

A Your mother gives you 'hand-me -down' clothes because I suspect she can't afford to buy new ones for you, especially since what she might buy for you this year, would not fit you next year. At your age you can't earn money to buy your own clothes, but there is no reason why (with your mother's permission) you shouldn't go to Charity Shops, and trade in the 'hand-me-downs' you don't like, for those of your own choice!

Q I know I killed my Grandma. I was very happy at home until Grandma came to stay. I love my Mum very much, and I used to sing round the house all day because I like singing and she liked to hear me. My Mum was very proud of my singing, and when Grandma moved in I heard my Mum telling her about the way I sang all over the house - so I never sang again. My Mum kept asking me to but I couldn't - not with *her* around. Grandma kept interfering in everything and I hated her being in the house all the time, and nothing was the same any more. One night my Dad was furious with me and sent me to bed, and then Grandma came into my bedroom and started trying to interfere. That night I prayed that she'd die, and the next morning I woke up and heard my mother

screaming that she was dead. They took her body away, but I can't go into her bedroom because I'm afraid of her ghost, because I killed her. I can never tell anyone what I did and I feel really bad and scared. Please help me.
Carole (9), Chiswick

A The first thing you must understand is that nobody can kill anybody or anything by wishing or praying that they should die - only actions can kill a living being! Sometimes when people are very angry and upset with each other, in the heat of the moment they will wish the other person were dead, but this wishing will not kill that person (however strongly they may feel at the time), and you certainly did not kill your Grandma! However much you resented your Grandma for disrupting your life by coming to live in your home, and however irritating she might have been by trying to 'interfere' between you and your parents, I am sure that she really loved you, otherwise she would not have concerned herself with your welfare. Therefore however scared you may feel that her ghost is haunting her bedroom, she would never want to do anything to harm you, and you have nothing to fear. Please try to believe that should there be any of your Grandma's presence left in your house, it is just memories of the happy thoughts and deeds that she tried so hard to think and do for you all. Please don't feel guilty about your relationship with your Grandma; just because we are related to someone, it does not mean that we always get on with them. Try to learn from this experience, and strive to be as kind and loving as you can to others in the future. It is essential that you talk to an adult about the way you are feeling at the moment, and if you go to Church, please have a word with the Priest who will put your mind at rest, and he will also not divulge your confidence in him. If you cannot talk to him, talk to your teacher, a close relative, your best friend's mother, or even phone the Samaritans - you really need to talk to someone!*

Q My mother is a saint and my father is terrible! My mother works really hard at home doing the cooking and cleaning and looking after my sister and me, and my father does nothing. My mother never goes to bed ill but last week she had such bad flu, the doctor made her stay in bed. My father made such a song and dance about looking after us all, and while I was helping him dust the living room I knocked over the vase of flowers on his grand piano. He went mad and said 'People like you should never have been born!' I started crying and eventually my mother had to get up and take over. I can't forget what he said, and how my mother couldn't even have one day ill in bed. I really hate him. Please help.

Hilary, London

A *Try not to be too hard on your father, because I expect he works very hard all day going out to work to earn money to support you all. Sometimes when people are tired and stressed out their tempers get short, and in the heat of the moment they say things that they really do not mean. I'm sure your father was really worried that your mother was so ill she had to stay in bed, and it all got too much for him - he's only human like the rest of us. If he was such a bad person your mother would be unhappy with him, and she would not put up with him. I'm sure that your father loves you very much and has probably forgotten what he said. If you feel brave enough, I think that you should tell him how sorry you are about upsetting the flowers and causing him extra work, but how upset you feel about what he said to you. Try to sort things out between you now, before the incident festers inside you and causes lasting damage with your relationship with your father.*

'That's Mine!'
Problems Between Siblings

Q My little sister keeps coming into my room and taking my toys. She throws all my things on the floor, and then *I* get told off for messing up my room! She's got lots of dolls and girl toys, but she won't play with them and just wants my cars and other things. I get told off if I hit her so how can I stop her?

Martin (11), Bexley

A *You shouldn't hit your little sister, and you can never fully stop anyone coming into your room if they really want to. Most boys think that girls' toys are silly, so how can you blame your sister for thinking the same thing too? Until you can both persuade your parents to give her toys that she would like to play with, why don't you lend her some of your toys so that she has no need to take them. I suspect that the real reason for her coming into your bedroom is because she wants to be with you and wants you to play with her. Maybe if you set aside a small amount of time each day to do neutral things together, like model making or painting, she would stop being desperate to be with you all the time, and she might even want to amuse herself in her own room.*

Q My Mum prefers my brother to me. He's 5 and I'm 9 and she cuddles him all the time and doesn't seem to notice I'm there unless I do something wrong and then she just shouts at me and tells me off. I'm always dropping things and I say all the wrong things, and I wish she loved me like she loves my brother. I sometimes think she doesn't love me at all and just thinks I'm a nuisance round the place. I'm really miserable, and even Dad's starting to have a go at me as he says I look 'sour faced' all the time. What should I do?
Jonathon, Chelsea

A Of course your Mum loves you just as much as your brother. The first thing you must do is cheer up. You will be amazed how much more attention and affection you will get once you have a happy smile on your face instead of a black look! Everyone likes to be with happy people, and most people try to keep away from miserable people. Your Mum must work very hard looking after you and your brother, and she probably gets very tired. So when you do wrong things around her, she shouts at you and tells you off because she really wants and needs your help, not your hindrance. However, just because you are the eldest brother, this does not mean that you don't need lots of cuddles, so tell your Mum how bad you've been feeling and ask her for a hug!

Q My sister is so pretty and so clever and works so hard that everyone says she'll go far in life. We're at the same school, and the teachers are always comparing us and telling me I should be more like my sister. Even my parents and their friends say why

can't I be more like her. Why should I be? She may be prettier and cleverer and work harder than me, but she's a horrid person! Why does no-one appreciate me?
Rachel (12), Herts

A It does not matter that others are cleverer than yourself, what matters is how hard you try at your work to achieve the best possible results for you. There will always be someone that people will say is 'prettier' than the rest of us, but remember that beauty comes from within. The most attractive people to be with are those who are at peace with themselves, who try hard to make others feel good, who are not jealous or envious of others but make the most of what they have - they have a beautiful personality. 'If you compare yourself to others you may become vain and bitter, for always there will be greater and lesser persons than yourself' (Desiderata) Those who are worse off will make you feel conceited and arrogant, and those who are better off will make you dissatisfied and unpleasant. I am sure that if you were to work harder, always try to do your very best, appreciate others and show everyone what a lovely person you are, life will start to get a little easier for you and you will be appreciated. You might also consider asking your parents if it would be possible for you to go to a different school where none of the teachers know your sister, and therefore could not make any comparisons between the two of you.

Q I'm 13 and the only girl in my family of 5 (I have 2 older brothers and 2 younger) and I'm fed up being the middle child. One minute my parents expect me to be responsible for and look after the little ones, and the other minute I'm not old enough to know my own mind or do my own thing. My parents are too busy working to notice I'm here half the time, the little ones rely on me to look after them but ignore me, and my older brothers think I'm too young to listen to or have anything to say. I never have any time for myself, I have no-one to talk to, no-one listens to my needs, and when I complain to my parents they say they are just working hard for me! I don't feel I fit in anywhere. What can I do?
Raju, Watford

A You'll soon be at an age when you will need time to study for exams as well time for yourself. If your parents won't listen to your needs you must talk to one of your teachers at school, explain the problem and see if they can have a chat with your parents. Your teacher needs to point out that although it is necessary for them to work hard to earn enough money to support the family, it cannot be at your expense. The responsibility for looking after your younger brothers must be shared throughout the family; indeed it might be better if one of your parents worked less and looked after you all, even if it means having a lower standard of living. However if this is not possible, your local Social Services may be able to help. Remember 'You are a child of the universe, no less than the trees and the stars: you have a right to be here.' (Desiderata)

Q I love the smell of old fireworks and I like looking at the pictures on the side of them. After Guy Fawkes night I searched around everywhere and collected a bag full of them, and brought them back home to play with. My older brother (who is always being mean to me and likes pushing me around) caught me playing with them and he grabbed them off me and threw them on the fire. One of them must have still been live because it went off with an enormous bang. All the soot came down the chimney, and there was such a mess that the room had to be redecorated. *I* got into really bad trouble with my parents and have been banned from playing with fireworks ever again. My older brother didn't get told off at all, although it was all his fault that the place was such a mess. How can I make my parents see how unfair they've been to me?
Keith (11) Staffs

A Your parents are being very fair to you - they are trying to keep you alive! It is extremely foolish to play with fireworks, and many children each year lose their eyesight, limbs and even their lives in so doing. Your older brother may well have saved your life by grabbing the fireworks off you, even if he was misguided enough to throw them on the fire. Don't moan at him - thank him, and try to find something less hazardous to play with next time!

'You're Not in Our Gang'
Problems Between Children

Q I'm really unhappy at school and I hate going there every day. The reason is that nobody wants me around and I'm not part of the gang. I have no-one to talk to at Break because they all go off and leave me, and I know they all snigger about me behind my back and call me a 'weed'. I try to tag along as much as I can, but they usually manage to lose me, and I feel awful being left on my own because I know the rest of the school knows that no-one wants to be my friend. I long for the end of the day when I can escape home. Please tell me how to get a friend.
Esther, Ashford

A There is no special formula that I can tell you, about how to get a friend. What I can tell you, is that I think your problem may be a considerable lack of confidence in yourself and your abilities. Be positive about yourself, and realise that you are just as good as anyone in the 'gang', and stop being so desperate to join it. Try to understand that if, for whatever reason, they don't want you to be part of their group at present, it is their loss - not yours! Concentrate on improving yourself at school with your school work, sport or musical abilities, and just try to excel at the things you know you are good at doing. Once the 'gang' know that you no longer need them, they will want you. Talk to your parents about the situation, or talk to a teacher that you feel you can trust. I'm sure that you will find there are many people in your life that like and love you, and they will be only too anxious to help you if you put your trust in them. Good luck - I know you'll win through.

Q I'm 12 years old, and there's a really clever girl in my class who tries to belittle me and make everyone else feel beneath her. It's difficult to decide whether or not to feel sorry for her because she doesn't do anything outside school except work all the time. Whenever my friends and I are talking to each other she interrupts us and corrects what we're saying. In fact we feel we can't

say *anything* around her in case she puts us down. No-one likes her, and although we try to avoid her she always seems to be around and it's driving us mad. What can we do?
Lucy, Richmond

A *This girl may be very clever, but she is also extremely insecure and needs to be wanted. She must know that none of you like her, and therefore she desperately wants your attention. Maybe if you actually asked for her opinions and gave her the attention she longs for, she would relax and be more pleasant to be with.*

Q I am good friends with Jane and Sally but only when there are two of us together. Whenever all three of us are around, both Sally and Jane are so anxious that they won't be the odd one out, I land up being left on my own. I get really hurt but neither of them seem to notice, and then when I am on my own again with either of them, each one behaves as if I am her best friend. What can I do?
Nicky, Southampton

A *I'm afraid that this is the old problem of 'two's company, three's a crowd'. As neither Jane nor Sally is mature enough to handle a 'threesome' friendship, you will have to try hard to find and introduce a fourth friend into your circle. In this way hopefully everyone will gain a little more confidence in themselves, and no-one will get left out!*

Q I'm an 11 year old boy, we've just moved house to another part of the country and I've started at a new school. I was really happy and had lots of friends at my old school, but I'm really unhappy at this new one. I'm short for my age and although I try not to eat too many sweets and fatty foods, I'm fat. My friends at my last school grew up with me and liked me for myself, but here the others boys pick on me and make fun of me. There's one boy in the class who is much bigger than anyone, and he leads the others

on to make life hell for me. I've tried to make friends and stand up for myself but it's just no good, I'm not big enough. I'm so unhappy I want to run away. Please help.
Prakash, Wembley

A *There is never any point in running away from a problem, it nearly always catches up with you again. You are doing exactly the right thing in trying to stand up for yourself and make friends, and these other boys are behaving in a particularly ignorant way and should be pitied. People who are unsure of themselves and lack something in their own personality, love to make others the butt of their 'jokes' - it makes them feel safe and superior. You can rise above them. You may be short and plump at the moment but this is only temporary, and very soon you will reach puberty, grow taller and lose your 'puppy fat'. Until then concentrate on improving your physique with lots of exercise and healthy food, and try to ignore any cruel comments. You are finding it difficult to cope with all this on your own at the moment, and I would advise you to have a word with a teacher that you feel you can trust. No teacher wants to have bullies in their school, and I am sure they will be only too willing to help you and to sort things out. You can also contact The Anti Bullying Campaign on 0171 378 1446, which is a helpline that you can ring for advice on any situation concerning bullying, and where you can talk to someone in confidence.*

Q My parents are not very well off and we live in a small house in a poor district. My father always wanted me to have the kind of education his parents could never afford to give him, and I have just got an assisted place at a very posh school. Both my parents are very proud of me, and although they will have to work hard to earn more money to support me, they don't mind and are very excited about it - but I am really scared. Up till now my friends have all come from similar backgrounds and homes such as mine, but now I will be with girls who have wealthy parents and live in big houses. How can I stop them finding out where I live, and how will I fit in with them when I am from such a different background? I'm worried sick, please help me.
Sandra, Hackney

A Don't be worried, your new school would not have chosen you if they were worried that you might not fit in with the other girls. It's not who you are in this life but what you yourself are like that counts. Be as proud of your parents and your home as they are of you, and be proud of your achievement. If you are not ashamed of your background and are as normal and friendly with new friends as you are with your present ones, they will accept you for yourself. If you appear to have something to hide, others will be suspicious of you and you will make life difficult for yourself. Be happy, accept this opportunity with enthusiasm and I'm sure you will have a great future ahead of you.

'Can I Be Excused?'
Problems Between Children and Teachers

Q There are thirty of us in my class at school and I sit at the back, and the teacher never seems to pay any attention to me or even notice that I am there half the time. She has her favourites in the class who get all her help and attention, and sometimes I have to ask to be excused just to prove my existence! What should I do?
Thelma, Ealing

A First of all, I suggest that you ask if you can move from the back of the class to the front. With so many pupils in the class for your teacher to attend to, you will get left out if you don't contribute more and make yourself known. Read up on the subject before your lesson, and become more involved by asking questions and showing interest. The more interest you show in her teaching, the more help and attention you will get from your teacher.

Q My teacher smokes like a chimney, and yet when he caught me smoking behind the gym he was furious and punished me. Is this fair?
Kevin, Maidstone

A Yes it is fair. Your teacher is an adult who has chosen to be hooked on a drug - smoking. He knows that you are not mature enough yet to make such a choice, and when he sees you smoking he probably wishes he had never even started. He knows the misery and health risks that smoking entails, and he does not want you to make the same mistakes as him. He also has a position of authority and responsibility towards his pupils. If you stop smoking now, in later years you may well owe him your life.

Q I'm a 13 year old girl, and I go to a co-ed school. My maths teacher is a 30 year old male, and although maths is my best subject and I know I am especially good at it, he gives much more of his attention to me than he does to any of the others in my class, and has even offered to give me extra coaching. All the boys have started saying there's no point in trying to get off with me because they don't stand a chance with my maths teacher around. My girlfriends say they're sure he fancies me. Could this be true, and if so what should I do?
Sophie, Chichester

A I doubt that a 30 year old male teacher, knowing that it would be illegal to do so, would want to get involved with a 13 year old girl. It is far more likely that, as a professional teacher, he is naturally proud of any gifted pupil and wants to help you reach as high a standard as possible, both for your sake and his reputation. The other pupils are probably just jealous of your talent and of all the attention this brings you. Do your very best in his lessons, and if you would like to have extra coaching because you feel it would help you, but you are worried about being alone with your teacher, suggest that he coaches others with you at the same time. Never give others less fortunate than yourself, the opportunity to destroy your chances in life.

Q I'm an 11 year old girl and I've got a crush on the games mistress. I want to be near her all the time and do things for her, and I love looking at her. I bring her little presents whenever I can and although she is always very friendly and chatty to me, I suspect I embarrass her - but I can't help myself. What should I do? Do you think I'm gay?
Anne, Wanstead

A No I don't think you are 'gay'; you are a normal young girl. Lots of children of your age have crushes on teachers of the same sex, it is just part of the growing up process. Your teacher will be used to receiving attention like this, but do try not to go 'over the top' with your presents. You are learning about your emotions, and the next stage will be crushes on pop stars, film stars and eventually boyfriends. Enjoy all stages of your life and learn from each experience.

Q I am 9 and go to a private boarding school which is one of the most respected in the country. The Head Master of the school keeps calling me into his office and makes me sit on his knee and touch him in funny places. My father is always telling me how lucky I am to go to this school so what should I do?
Jason, Langley

A Tell your father or mother at once what is happening! If you afraid of telling them, you must phone CHILDLINE on 0800 1111. It is very important *that you tell them as soon as possible.*

'Inge Gave Us an Ice-Cream'
Problems with Au Pairs/Nannies

Q I feel like I'm in competition with my Au Pair for my children's affections, and I don't like it. I am a single parent having to work long hours and not getting to be with my children as much as I would like, and therefore I am obviously pleased that they are very happy with her when I am not around. I have always made a point never to undermine my Au Pair's authority with them, by telling them that they can do something (even if I wanted them to) when she has just told them they can't. However she is not doing the same for me. I have told her time and time again how I wish my children to be brought up, what they can and can't do, but I continually find that my wishes are not being carried out. When I'm around and tell them not to do things, they say things like 'but Inge lets us do this' or ' but Inge gave us an ice-cream' and then they get upset with me and think that I'm just around to spoil their fun. When she comes in the room they rush to her and ignore me, and I'm made to feel in the way. It's as if they feel they are being disloyal to her if they show affection for me! I'm afraid that she is eroding my role as a mother and my authority with my children, by deliberately spoiling them. I feel guilty that I'm thinking this way because I don't want to make my children unhappy, but I am getting increasingly unhappy with the situation. What should I do?
Suzanne, Highgate

A You are being more than fair to your Au Pair, and it is admirable the way you always put your children's happiness and well being before your own, but I do not think that she is being fair to you. You are her employer, and as such she must respect your wishes with regard to the way you want your children to be disciplined. Your children must be made to understand that Au Pairs come and go, but you will always be there for them. If she continues to spoil them and undermine your authority, your unhappiness with the situation will filter through and they will not be happy children. Most working mothers feel guilty that they do not spend enough time with their children, and it is naturally difficult to see them give the 'substitute' a lot of affection.

However, anyone looking after your children should be sensitive to your feelings and do her utmost not to try to steal your children's affections away from you. At some time in the not too distant future your Au Pair will leave to go home and your children will be upset, therefore if she refuses to respect your wishes the sooner she leaves the better.

Q Please, please help. I recently became Au Pair to a very wealthy family in Chelsea. Last night I heard the little girl of the house crying, so I went to her room to comfort her. As I got to the door I saw her father touching parts of her he should not. I am sure her mother has no idea, what can I do? I am so worried for the little girl, but I need the job so much.
Sanja, Chelsea

A *First of all confront the father and tell him what you saw. See how he responds, and if you are still convinced that he was abusing his daughter, no job is more important than the welfare and safety of a child. If you are right in your suspicions, you must help this little girl by alerting others to the situation. If you got your job through an Au Pair Agency, give them a call and ask them to sort the situation out for you. If you got your job through an advert or through friends, phone CHILDLINE on 0800 1111 and let them sort things out. Don't worry that you will be out of a job - I can assure you that there are plenty more families who would be delighted to welcome such a caring and responsible Au Pair into their home.*

Q I am 16 years of age but I have a crush on my Au Pair. I watch her undress through the crack in the door, and I have sexy dreams about her. I think I will die if I don't sleep with her. She has really been employed for my little sister who is 9: Kristina is 22. What can I do?
Justin, Knightsbridge

A *Feelings such as those that you are now experiencing for Kristina are entirely natural in a boy of your age. However, she* has as much right to be treated with respect as your mother or sister, and it is disrespectful to watch her undress through a crack in the door. I am sure that if she catches you doing this, she will not only be extremely upset and angry, she will tell your parents and you will find yourself in a lot of trouble! Kristina is a member of your household and you should not contemplate playing around on 'your own doorstep'. Go out a little more with your friends to take your mind off her, and remember that Au Pairs only stay with a family for a short while. The more you can keep your feelings for her under control now, the easier it will be for you when she eventually leaves.

QI am a live-in Nanny to two adorable little boys,and have become very close to the whole family. Over the last six months it has become very apparent to me that the husband and wife are not very close. I have fallen in love with him, and I know that I would make a better mother to his children than her. I have seen him looking at me and I'm sure he feels the same way too. What should I do?
Jessie, Barnes

AI think that you should remember the basic rules of being a Nanny, and the terms of your employment with this family. Being a Nanny can be a heart breaking business, and as much as you would like them to be, the children in your charge can never belong to you - they are in your temporary care as long as their parents wish them to be, and then it's 'good-bye'! Whatever troubles there are between the husband and wife, it is their business, and you were not employed to make matters worse. In fact, part of your job is to ensure the smooth running of the home, the children, and the general harmony of the whole family. I think that it would be folly indeed to imagine that, if the husband is looking at you with more interest than usual, he is thinking anything other than having a quick fling on the side! Fathers very rarely go off with their Nanny mistress. Concentrate on finding your own available boyfriend, instead of trying to take someone else's husband and children. If you find this too difficult for you, change your job and save yourself and everyone else a load of heartache.

Q Please help. I am 12 and I love my mother and father very much. I woke up last night and saw my father kissing Marianna the Au Pair in the kitchen while my mother was out. Should I tell my father I saw him or shall I tell my mother? I don't know what to do.
Jack, Belgravia

A *I think you should confront your father and tell him what you saw. Tell him how upset and confused you feel about the situation and that you don't know whether to tell your mother. See what he has to say, and then let him sort things out - hopefully everything will be back to normal in your home very soon.*

TEENAGERS

'You Don't Love Me'
Boys' Problems and The Problems
They Have with Girls

Q My girlfriend baffles me. We have been going out for 10 months (she's 17 and I'm 19) and I take her everywhere. We see each other nearly every night and I phone her twice a day, but recently all I hear her say is 'You don't love me!' I admit that I have never told her that I do, because I don't know myself, and when she asks where our relationship is going I am always honest and say 'I don't know'. We have always had a really good time together, lots of fun and laughs, so what's her problem now? I really care about her but all this is getting on my nerves. Could she be trying to get me to marry her?
Mark, Islington

A Your girlfriend, for whatever reason, is feeling insecure, and needs reassurance from you that you are not going to leave her and that you have a future together. She wants more from the relationship than you are prepared to give her at present, and she may want to marry you, but I think that you are both very young to consider getting married, and if you have any doubts at all about your future together you should not contemplate it. Tell your girlfriend that no-one knows what is going to happen tomorrow, and that she should enjoy what she has at present, not wasting any of it by spending her time worrying about the future. You are being as honest as you can with her, and you certainly wouldn't spend so much time with her, if you didn't care a great deal for her. If she can't be satisfied with this, and can't wait to see what life may bring, then maybe you should consider having a break to decide what you both want, before you get so fed up with the present situation that it all ends in tears!

Q A few months ago I picked up a girl at a disco, and after I had taken her home I decided I didn't want to see her again. I didn't know how to reject her and I didn't want to hurt her feelings, so I gave her a false name and telephone number. She really wanted to meet me again and I didn't know how to get out of it, so I arranged to meet her the next week for a drink and stood her up! She found out my real name and phone number from my friends and keeps ringing me up. I'm running out of excuses, what shall I do?
Simon, Putney

A *Be honest with her, and always have the courage in future to tell someone in a sensitive way, without hurting their feelings, that they are not your sort. You will cause far less damage this way, than if you just evade the issue and hope it will go away!*

Q I'm 18, male, and started as a student at University this term. I have never been to a fee-paying school and never left home before, and here I am surrounded by Public School boys. They are all so socially aware and confident, and I feel like the poor cousin, left out, inadequate and unsure of myself. How am I going to deal with all this?
Adrian, Norwich

A *First of all you should remember the purpose of you going to University. You are there to gain knowledge and generally better yourself in life. Hold your head up high and prove yourself in your work, and people will begin to look up to you. If you are good at it, concentrate on sport as it is an excellent equaliser. Observe and absorb the good points of everyone you meet, and bear in mind that others will only value you as much as you value yourself.*

Q I'm at a boys' boarding school with a strong military tradition, and girls are allowed to join the school in the sixth form. I have been in the sixth form for a year now, and I have never had a girlfriend. I make a mess of every attempt to go out with girls; I am feeling more and more useless and my work is suffering more than ever; I keep thinking 'Why would any of them want me anyway?' One of my Form Masters used to tell me that I couldn't do anything properly, and his favourite phrase to me was ' You are a waste of space and will never amount to anything'! I'm a bit of a loner nowadays, and I spend a lot of time thinking instead of doing because I know I'll mess up anyway. I'm depressed and I need some advice.
Richard, Glos.

A *You must stop thinking so much about girls - the more you want them, the less likely you are to get them. Try treating girls as ordinary people and just be friends with them. You will find throughout life that very often relationships develop from friendships. Concentrate on developing good friendships with the other boys, go round in a group and have some fun. I am sure that your Form Master was probably following a military tradition of character building by putting you down, to make you try harder. However this is a particularly ignorant way to behave and you should pity him. Try to build up your confidence by making a list of all your good points and achievements, read more, get lots of exercise, and just remember that we all have a talent for something.*

Q My girlfriend and I are both 18 and she is always accusing me of being jealous and possessive over her, and I know she's right but I just can't stop myself. Whenever she says she's seeing her girlfriends I can't stop myself cross-questioning her about it, and when we're out together I feel a mixture of terror and rage inside me if she smiles at another boy or talks to them. Sometimes the feelings are so strong that I have to leave her, and it takes days before I am recovered enough to speak to her again. I know she'll get really fed up soon and leave me. How can I handle the way I feel?
David, Mddx.

A *Jealousy is an insecurity in ourselves, and a feeling that we are worth a lesser amount of love and respect than others, and that other people are more important than us. Jealousy is also a lack of trust, not only in ourselves but in the other person, and no relationship can survive without trust on both sides. Jealousy is allowing the other person's behaviouro cause you emotional discomfort. If you really liked yourself you would not get upset when your girlfriend chooses to be with others. The way to handle it is to recognise that jealousy is a put-down of yourself, and if you can love, like and believe in yourself, you won't need the love and approval of anyone else to give you a sense of value. If your girlfriend chooses to be with her friends or talk to other boys, it is her choice and absolutely no reflection on you or your worth. Try to understand that jealousy is a wasteful emotion which prevents you from enjoying the present moment, and each present moment is the only important moment of your life.*

Q I'm 16 and I've only ever got to kiss one girl, and that was two years ago. I don't feel ugly, I don't dress badly, I don't smell, but I never get to kiss girls at parties or anywhere else! My friends are always 'teasing' me about it and they just put more pressure on me to do something about it. I need your advice.
Andrew, Milton Keynes

A *Relax and take it easy! So what if you're not kissing the girls at present, you've got a lifetime ahead of you to kiss them. Concentrate on yourself, and in achieving the best possible results you can get both in work and in sporting activities. When you are with girls treat them as friends and be a good listener, because if they think you are just after 'one thing' they will 'run a mile'. Remember that self-sufficiency is attractive, neediness is not.*

'Aw C'mon - Everyone Else Does It' Girls' Problems and The Problems They Have with Boys

Q My boyfriend is really putting the pressure on me to sleep with him, and keeps telling me 'everyone else does it' and that it's just the natural and normal thing to do. I really like him but I'm not sure if I really want to go to bed with him yet. I'm frightened of losing him if I don't, so what should I do?
Sarah, Slough

A *If it's natural and normal for them - fine, but if it's not for you at present, don't do it! Having sex with someone just because everyone else is doing it, is not the sensible way to behave and will just destroy your self respect and possibly cheapen your relationship. If your boyfriend leaves you because he can't persuade you to do something against your will, then he does not care enough about* you, *and you are better off without him!*

Q I am 15 and I started going out with a boy 3 months ago, and I really love him. The other night I told him that I loved him, but instead of saying it back he went really quiet, and I haven't heard from him since. One of his mates says he doesn't want to see me any more. I don't understand what's wrong, what can I do?
Lesley, Essex

A *It's important to realise the difference between sexual attraction and real love, and I feel that after just three months of going out with someone it is more likely to be lust than love. There is nothing you can do if this boy doesn't contact you, and tells his mates that he doesn't want to see you any more. He obviously just wanted to be friends with you and was not ready to make a commitment, and he is also not mature enough to tell you so. However, look on the bright side - at least he was decent enough not to take advantage of your feelings for him.*

Q Last night I went with some friends to a disco and had a few dances with a boy who asked for my telephone number. I didn't know what to do so I gave it to him. Today I can't really remember much about him as it was quite dark in the disco. I've never been out on a date before and I don't know whether I should agree to see him if he phones up. If I did go out with him, does he pay or do I? I really don't know what to do.
Jayne, Bexleyheath

A Stop worrying, he may never ring! If he does, arrange to meet him in the daylight in a public place and see what you think. As you are unsure about this boy, and you also know nothing at all about him, I think you should pay your half share to avoid any misunderstandings about implied obligations. Indeed, I think it makes sense to apply this as a rule to any casual dates you may have in the future. Don't give your telephone number to boys unless you are really sure that you want to - take theirs instead, and then make up your own mind in your own time as to whether you want to see them again.

Q I'm 16 years old and I've recently started going round with a group of friends, and have been introduced to a really nice guy who I know fancies me. In the times we've met we've got on really well, and I find it easy to talk to him. The problem is I don't fancy him. I know he wants to ask me out, but is it fair on him to accept?
Jasmin, Royston

A If and when this guy asks you out, you tell him that you are very happy to go out with him on a friendship basis and do not lead him on, then it is fair on him to accept. You might find that as you get to know him better as a friend, you start to fancy him. If not, you can have a good time together as friends, and through meeting his other friends, you might be introduced to someone you do fancy. There are great benefits to be had from platonic friendships with people of the opposite sex - it is a joy that not everyone is able to experience.

Q I'm 15 and I hate using sanitary towels. I find them uncomfortable especially when I'm playing games, I can't swim when I'm wearing them, and I hate wearing trousers because I am sure everyone can see them when I have my period. Lots of my friends use tampons and they tell me I should too, but I'm scared of trying to use them, and I've also heard that they can cause thrush and toxic shock syndrome. Please give me some advice.
Anita, Sevenoaks

A *So long as you change the tampons regularly, there is minimal chance of getting toxic shock syndrome or thrush. You could try going to a female doctor for advice, or there is usually a helpline for the tampon company that you can call. If you are worried about how to use them, there is an explicit leaflet inside each box to help you. If after seeking advice you are still scared of using tampons, you will find that there are many ultra-thin towels in the shops now, that are fairly inconspicuous under tight clothes.*

Q I'm taller than all my friends and I feel I stick out like a sore thumb. I'm shy and I don't like the attention that my height gives me. For example, when I go to parties I feel intimidated because the boys notice me first, whilst I would rather they chatted up my friends first so that I could stay in the background until I felt more confident. I don't really want to go out much now because I'm so self conscious about my appearance and I've lost all my confidence. Please help me.
Karon, Edinburgh

A *Walk tall and be proud of your height - even wear high heels! Boys love tall girls, small girls long to be tall, and remember that tall girls will always look twice as elegant as short girls. Never stoop to try to make yourself appear shorter, you will only injure your neck and back. When you are in your 20's you will appreciate this gift, when boys notice and appreciate your looks. There will probably come a time when you will wish you were even taller!*

'You're Never in When I Call'
Problems Between Friends

Q I really miss my best friend. We used to do everything together, but since she got a boyfriend I hardly ever see her. Even when she's not seeing 'him', she doesn't want to go out in case he phones! When I do see her, she only wants to talk about 'him' anyway. I've tried to talk to her about how upset I am but she says I'm just jealous of her. Now she's never 'in' when I call, although I know she must be. I feel really lonely and hurt that she has just 'dropped' me. What can I do?
Alison, Cambridge

A *Friends are for ever, boyfriends may not be, and you should never fall out with a friend over a boy. When you eventually speak to her again, ask her if her boyfriend has any friends he could introduce you to, then maybe on occasions you could all go out together. Life changes, and it was bound to happen that one or both of you would find a boyfriend and need some independence from the other, it's part of growing up. Let her know that when she needs you, you will be there for her, and then start trying to develop some new friendships of your own.*

Q I'm really worried about my girlfriend; she's getting thinner every time I see her and she looks really ill. She seems to be really nervy all the time and either says she's not hungry and doesn't want to eat a thing when we go out, or she eats everything in sight as if this is the last meal she will ever get! I stayed the night at her parents' house last week, and during the night she kept getting up and going to the bathroom. I'm sure I heard her being sick, but when I asked her about it she said she was fine. I don't think she's 'fine', what shall I do?
Katie, Dulwich

A I suspect that your friend is suffering from Bulimia, which is a food disorder where someone alternately starves themselves for days, and then gorges on as much food as they can find, deliberately making themselves sick afterwards. Your girlfriend is on a dangerous course and needs help as soon as possible. Urge her to go and see her local GP who will be able to help. He will probably refer her for counselling, because there must be some problem in her life that she is trying to avoid coming to terms with, and in which she feels she is out of control. This leads her to concentrate all her attention and energies on food, and then to control it's intake. If she will not go to her doctor, you must let her know that as you are so concerned about her you will have to tell her parents - you are not being disloyal, you are being a true friend. If you would like further advice call The Eating Disorders Association Helpline on 01603 621414 (for over 18's) or 01603 765050 (for under 18's).

Q I'm studying for my A levels and my best friend Carol, who is a lot cleverer than I am, kept telling me that I was spending too much time with my boyfriend and I wouldn't pass the exams if I didn't stop seeing him for a while. I got myself in a state and kept putting my boyfriend off until finally he left me. Now I find *she's* going out with him! I'm really upset, what do I do?
Helen, Northants

A Get rid of your 'best friend' and concentrate on your studies! Also learn a lesson from this escapade, that you can never trust the motives of girl friends when they 'slag off' your boyfriend. They may either want your company solely for themselves as a playmate to go around with, or they may want him! Seek your own counsel on matters of the heart, and listen to your own instincts.

Q My best friend smells of B.O., what should I do? Should I slip a deodorant into her bag and hope she takes the hint, or should I just tell her? Please advise.
Andrea, Caerphilly

A Please don't slip a deodorant into her bag, that would be
cruel in the extreme. Be a good friend to her and just tell her - she
may be embarrassed that you had to tell her, but will be very grateful
that you did. She is used to her own body odour and obviously doesn't
know that it offends other people, otherwise she would be buying her
own deodorant.

Q Every time my girlfriend goes out with someone, she
ends it really quickly because she's frightened they will end it
before she does! She's just met someone she really does like and
their relationship is really good, but she's worried that he's just using
her and she can't finish their relationship because she's really keen
on him. Sometimes he's really 'off' with her, but every time she
asks him why he's being like that, he says there's nothing wrong.
She's getting more and more anxious that he's going to give her up
any minute. What should my friend do?
Claire, Kingston

A Your friend is on a self-destruct course, and unless she
relaxes, stops putting pressure on him, and enjoys the relationship
he will give her up! Sometimes when we like someone too much and
think we are not good enough to keep their attention (which means that
eventually they will have to leave us), we subconsciously sabotage our
own relationship, so that in the end when they do leave we were proved
right!

Q I'm really worried about my friend. We're both 15, and
we've been inseparable since childhood, going everywhere and
doing everything together. However now I don't seem to know her
anymore, she has changed so much. She hardly eats anything, her
complexion is terrible, her eyes look glazed, and she seems to be
generally spaced out and on a different planet to me most of the
time. She always wants to be on her own in her bedroom, because
she says she wants some peace and quiet. I've been to a few parties
with her where she's gone wild, and she's smoked cannabis. I want
my *old* friend back. What should I do?
Tanya, Redditch

A It sounds like your friend could have a drug problem, and although she would probably react unfavourably if you take a moralistic stand with her, she needs your help and to know that you will always there for her as a friend. Taking drugs will eventually kill her, apart from it being illegal, and I recommend you to call the National Drugs 24 hour Helpline on 0800 776600. All calls to them are confidential and they will advise you what to do.

'You're Too Young Anyway'
Problems Between Parents and Children/Children's Boyfriends/Girlfriends

Q I'm a responsible 16 year old and my boyfriend's 17, and we've been dating now for two months. We go out a lot with friends and to parties but we never seem to get to get a chance to be alone together for more than a few minutes. Both our houses are bustling with people, and if we go to his room or mine and close the door to listen to tapes, we can be sure that within minutes a parent will be knocking on the door demanding to know what is going on! It's so embarrassing that we are never allowed any privacy at all. When I complained to my mother last week, all she could say to me was 'You're too young anyway!' Any suggestions?
Anthea, Bristol

A I can understand that, although she knows you are not underage to have sex with your boyfriend, your mother is concerned about your welfare. You need to explain to her that if both of you really wanted to have sex you could find somewhere to do it, in the back of a car or on a walk in the woods for example. Explain that you have too much respect for her wishes to have sex in her house, but that you just wish to have some privacy sometimes. However, you will want to have a sexual relationship one day, and rather than having to lie to her you would prefer to be open and honest about it, and be able to ask for her advice.

Q I'm 17 and I want to sleep with my boyfriend. I would like to go on the pill, not only because I don't want to get pregnant, but because I would like to have a bigger bust! The problem is that my parents are dead against sex before marriage, and they even wrote letters of objection to my school when they heard we were being given lessons on sex because they thought we were too young! I don't want to deceive them but I can never talk to them about contraception, so what should I do?
Rebecca, Somerset

A First of all accept your bust as it is - at 17 your body is still not fully developed. Small can be beautiful, and your boyfriend obviously doesn't object! There are may be other side effects to going on the pill, and you need to discuss the possible dangers fully with your local GP, or your local Family Planning Clinic where you will find very caring people willing to listen and talk to you. Of course you could always buy a packet of condoms!

Q I am an 18 year old male and image conscious, and I like to make an effort in how I look. However, my parents don't always see eye to eye with my 'fashion trends'. I desperately want to have my ears pierced, just one, and they are forbidding me to have it done. They seem to think that only gays or hooligans have pierced ears, which of course I know isn't the case. I don't want to offend them too much as I still live at home, but I *am* at an age where I want to assert my independence and be myself. I don't feel this is such a big issue, but am I being unreasonable?
Niall, Dublin

A I don't think that you are being unreasonable, but obviously your parents do. As you are not yet independent of them and still live in their home, I think you should respect their wishes and give in this time. When you eventually move out, you will be free to abuse your ears as much as you wish!

Q My girlfriend's parents don't approve of me socially because my father used to work for them as their chauffeur. Although they are polite, they are very false and I am made to feel unwelcome. This is very hard for my girlfriend as she feels torn between me and her parents, and we always end up arguing about them. We love each other very much, but all this is putting a strain on our relationship. What can I do?
Trevor, York

A *Basically there is not a lot you can do except give your girlfriend all the love and support you can, and stop taking the frustrations you have with her parents' behaviour out on her, by having fruitless arguments. For whatever reasons, her parents disapprove of you, and may not even like you very much. So what? If you are both happy together then that is all that matters - we can't all be liked and approved of by everyone in this life, however much we might like to be. Try to keep your visits to her parents' house to a minimum, and when you are there, be as pleasant as possible to them for your girlfriend's sake. Who knows, maybe one day they might change their minds about you!*

Q When my daughter was 16 she vowed that she would never marry and that she hated men. Last year on her 17th birthday she came home and announced that she was pregnant. Eventually, through days and nights of heart searching and talks with me late into the night, she decided to have an abortion. She is now 18, and ever since the termination she has blamed me for 'making' her get rid of the baby, and she no longer talks to me and wants to leave home. I am at my wits end; she lost her baby and it seems I've lost my daughter! What can I do?
Celia, Bath

A *Many women undergo enormous feelings of guilt and suffer from depression after an abortion. Although your daughter decided to have an abortion, she now can't take responsibility for her actions and has to blame someone else - and unfortunately that someone is you. During those 'days and night of heart searching and talks' with her, you expressed your opinions as to what your daughter should do.*

However, your daughter has a mind of her own and she didn't have to take your advice. Your daughter needs help, and I would advise you to get her to see your local GP as soon as possible, and he will refer her for much needed counselling. You will need to be patient, resilient and supportive with your daughter and eventually, with professional help, she will come back to you.

Q I'm a 15 year old girl who's recently started wearing glasses, and I look really awful in them. I take them off before I go to parties because I look so bad, but then I look stupid because I keep bumping into things and I can't see my friends clearly! I desperately want to wear contact lenses but my parents say I'm too young. These glasses are ruining my social life, what can I do?
Louise, Rochester

A *First of all you should understand how attractive women can look wearing glasses, provided they are ones that suit them. There may be medical reasons why a girl of your age cannot wear contact lenses, and you need to ask your optician if this is the case - if it is, then choose some attractive new frames that really suit you. If the reason is not a medical one, and they merely think that you may lose expensive contact lenses, you can point out to them that there are excellent disposable ones on the market which are very reasonably priced.*

Q I'm a 19 year old male and all my mates have at some time had quite long relationships with girls, some for 6 months or more, and they have taken their girlfriends home to meet their parents. I've had girlfriends but none of them have been serious enough relationships for me to introduce them to my parents, and I haven't wanted to. Last week I was having a conversation with them, and reading between the lines I realised that they think I'm gay! I'm too embarrassed to talk to them about it, so how do I convince them I'm not?
Tony, Camden

A You don't have to convince them; just set their minds at rest as to what your sexual preferences are, and forget it. Not everyone needs the company of the opposite sex, and this does not make them 'gay'. You don't make a big 'song and dance' about taking your male friends home, so why not treat your female friends in the same way, and let them visit the place where you live in a normal manner - not as a potential wife!

Q I am 40 years old and have been going out with a younger man who is 26. Although there is a large age difference between us, we have been very happy and I am in love with him. I have a 19 year old daughter who does not live with me, and yesterday my boyfriend told me that they have been meeting each other, have fallen in love and want to get married! I am distraught; I am torn between love for my daughter and her happiness, and my love for my boyfriend. What shall I do?
Gill, Wentworth

A My heart goes out to you - this is an appalling situation. However, if your daughter and your boyfriend are truly in love, there is not a lot you can do except to wish them well. You will need to summon up all your courage to get you through the following months, especially if you are to help your daughter with her wedding plans. If you can, take a holiday and try to sort out your emotions while you are away from them both. Be brave, and I'm sure that eventually you will find joy in seeing your daughter so happy.

DATING

'You're Never Ready on Time'
Problems Men Have with Women

Q I have to keep to tight schedules because of my job, and therefore when I make arrangements to meet my girlfriend for a date I always make an effort to be there on time. However she's always late, and she can't understand why I get so angry and upset with her. I feel her disregard for punctuality shows a lack of respect for me, especially since when I say 'You're never ready on time' she never has a good reason for her lateness. Surely if she really cared for me she would want to keep me happy?
Gavin, Boston, USA

A *Your girlfriend obviously has a completely different attitude to yours on punctuality and has probably got into the habit of being late for everything in her life, not just you. She may think that if you really cared for her, you would be more understanding towards her and not give her a such a hard time when she's late. However if your feelings were really important to her, she would make a supreme effort to be on time for you. If punctuality is the only cause of dispute in your relationship and you still want to go out with her, make the meeting time for your date an hour earlier than you want it to be. Hopefully then you will both arrive at the same time and life will become less stressed and happier for you both.*

Q I was at University with Sue and we went out together for six months. We broke up after a trivial row and graduated soon after. It's now a year since I've seen her and I can't get her out of my mind. I found out her address and telephone number, and although I've written to her and tried phoning her, she doesn't answer my letters or return my calls. As she shares a flat with other girls I know she's not married, and so I know there's still hope for me. I'm desperate to be with her again, what shall I do next?
Rob, Cardiff

A *I'm sorry to sound brutal, but there is nothing more you can do. If she does not want to return your calls or answer your letters, you have to face the fact that she is no longer interested in seeing you again. Maybe she already has a meaningful relationship; maybe she's engaged to be married. Just because you feel strongly attracted to someone it does not necessarily mean that they feel the same way about you. Don't feel rejected, there's nothing wrong with you. Just face the fact that this particular relationship, for whatever reason, did not work out - enjoy the memory and move on. Life is for living in the present, and not for wasting precious present moments hankering after things that may have been. You are young, and if you open up your eyes to other possibilities you never know who might suddenly appear on the scene. The unknown can be an exciting prospect; make the most of every opportunity and make sure you live your life to the full. This life is not a rehearsal, it's the only* performance!

Q I have had a succession of failed relationships over the past three years, and wonder what I have been doing wrong. All my girlfriends have lived abroad or at least a hundred miles away from me. I've tried meeting and dating local girls but I never seem to fancy them. I really want to settle down, but things are just not working out. Help!
Roy, Hendon

A *You say you want to settle down but I wonder if you really do. You may in fact be someone who is committed to non-commitment. It may be that the reason you find girls who live a ridiculously long way away from you attractive, is because subconsciously you know that the distance between you will eventually cause the relationship to break up, meaning that you will not have to commit yourself. Finding an attractive girl who lives just around the corner would be far too dangerous, as it would be much harder to find excuses as to why you couldn't commit yourself to her. Just be honest with yourself and decide what you really want. It's not a crime to want to stay single, but it's dishonest to lead a partner on and deceive them as to your true intentions.*

Q I am 38 years old and have been having an affair with two women for more than a year. I can't decide which of them I really want, and am exhausted leading this double life. I am sure that one of them will find out about the other soon and I might lose them both. I have never had just one relationship at a time and I think I may have a problem. What do you think?
Des, Surbiton

A I think you have been behaving disgracefully to both your girlfriends and don't deserve either of them! Maybe you should consider having professional counselling to find out why you cannot handle one relationship at a time, and why you need the danger and excitement of a second one to give you your kicks. We all have to grow up some time, and maybe now *is the time for you.*

Q My girlfriend and I met through a singles organisation and have been seeing each other now for 18 months. Although we agreed, when we started going out, not to attend any more of their functions, I recently found an up-to-date events list in her bedroom, and she makes excuses not to see me when I now know they are holding their functions. I asked her whether she is going to them, and she denied it. I don't believe her. What do I do now?
Gary, New York, USA

A Sometimes the best advice comes from oneself! If all your instincts tell you that your girlfriend is lying, then you are probably right. Maybe, in order to find out the truth, you should attend the next singles function without telling your girlfriend that you are going to be there. However, you have to be certain that you can cope with the consequences: public confrontation if she is there also: explanations you would have to give her if she isn't, but subsequently found out that you were! Basically no relationship is worth having unless there is trust between the two of you.

Q I have always been attracted to tall, slim, leggy women. However I've finally met someone I really enjoy being with, but she is short and stocky! I am torn between whether I should continue with this relationship, or whether I should seek someone I am more attracted to. Please advise.
Hans, Dusseldorf

A *How successful have your relationships been with tall, slim, leggy women? If they have been less than successful, then maybe it's a change for the better to go out with a short stocky woman whose company you really enjoy. If you continue to enjoy her company, then maybe one day you will be surprised to find out how attractive she has become to you! Compatibility between the most successful couples does not just rely on physical attraction. Few people get to choose the type they fall in love with, it just happens, and very often it's not the sort of person they thought they were looking for. This could well be the turning point in your life!*

Q I've just met a gorgeous woman I'm really attracted to, and I know she feels the same way about me. I'd like to start a relationship with her but I'm wary about getting involved as she has two young children, and I have never wanted to be involved with someone else's children. I really don't know what to do, I need some suggestions.
Bjorn, Malmo

A *As you have realised, if you get involved with this woman you will eventually be involved with her children - she comes as a package deal. I suggest you go out with her a few times and then, if you are still getting on well, ask to meet the children and have a few outings with them as a family. If you find you like the children and they like you, then give the relationship a try. You never know, you might even end up really enjoying the whole situation!*

Q I'm sleeping on a fairly regular basis with a girl who works for me. She's made it clear that she wants a committed relationship, and I've tried to make it clear that I don't! I know I should stop sleeping with her as our affair cannot lead to anything, but I'm worried that if I do, it will affect our working relationship which is so good. Please help.
Christopher, Wapping

A Deep down inside us, we all know what is right and what is wrong, and what we should or shouldn't do. If you really feel you should stop sleeping with your girlfriend, for whatever reason you may have, every time you do sleep with her you are leading her on and giving her false hopes. The break-up of your sexual relationship probably will affect your working relationship, however you should always follow your instincts as to what is the right thing to do.

Q I have known a woman as a friend for the past seven years, and I would consider her to be my best friend. She has had a constant stream of boyfriends during this time, and I have had many girlfriends too. Recently she became single again, and my feelings have become so strong for her that I desperately want to tell her how I feel. She constantly refers to me as her 'best friend' and tells me how wonderful our friendship is. If I make a move, I feel I will risk ruining the wonderful friendship we have formed over the years. Do you think I should stay silent and lonely?
Gordon, Dumfries

A I personally believe that the best foundation anyone could ever have for a relationship, comes from being best friends. Start asking her out on dates, and without making any amorous advances towards her, gently move your friendship onto a different footing. Then one night over dinner (in a romantic setting), tell her how much you value the friendship between you, how you now find you have even deeper feelings for her, and ask her how she feels towards you. If she says she just values you as a friend, accept her answer and assure her that you won't mention the subject again. If however she intimates that she feels more for you too, then you have a good chance of a very rosy future ahead for both of you.

Q My best friend Jim has just been done for drunk driving. Through the grapevine I have been told that my girlfriend Sue, who said she was having a night out with the girls, was caught with him in the car. She has not told me anything about this; she just said what a good time she'd had with the girls. What should I do?
Geoff, Brentford

A How reliable is your grapevine source of information? Even if the story is true, there could be an innocent reason for your girlfriend being in the car, and she may feel embarrassed to tell you. This is obviously an important issue for you, and you need to know the truth as soon as possible. Stop torturing yourself and confront them both as soon as possible. If there is a plausible explanation, then you will have diffused a potentially explosive situation building up in your mind, and being blown out of all proportion. However if you find out that they have been deceiving you, then you will be well rid of them both!

Q I'm 28 and have been going out with Jan for two years, but I know in my heart of hearts that things are not right although I am extremely fond of her. Three weeks ago I met Erica through work, and we have met for lunch several times and had dinner together. She's as keen on me as I am on her, and although I've been honest with her about my relationship with Jan, I haven't told Jan about Erica. I don't want to tell Jan about her in case I burn my bridges, and find myself left with neither of them if things don't work out with Erica. Please advise me.
Laus, Norway

A Well, if you carry on in the way you are at the moment, you are in great danger of 'burning your bridges' with both of them. Erica will probably not be content to stay as 'the other woman' for too long, and Jan is bound to notice a change in your attitude towards her and eventually find out about Erica. If you know that things are not right between you and Jan, and you are keen on Erica, then it would be best to be honest with Jan and end the relationship. Two years is long enough to find out whether or not she is the right girl for you, so why not give a 100% of your effort into trying to make a successful relationship with Erica and see what happens. If things don't work out you are young enough to meet someone else - at least you will be able to live with your conscience!

Q Ten years ago I had a brief affair with Karen, and I was upset when she ended it. We have always kept in touch, and now she is going out with someone she calls 'Mr Nice-but-Dim'! Recently in various subtle ways she has tried to ascertain my feelings for her, and has jokingly suggested that we should get married in a few years time if neither of us has found anyone else! I am still crazy about her and I know she is not satisfied with Mr NBD. Why didn't she say the things she is saying to me now, nine months ago when we were both free, and why didn't I announce my feelings for her then? Why do people never say what they feel at the right time? Do people become more attractive to you when they are going out with someone else; am I more attractive to her now that she is dissatisfied with Mr NBD? Should I tell her how I feel and maybe risk losing her as a friend and getting hurt again?

Steve, Dunstable

A *Who knows why any of us say the things we do at any given point in time. Maybe she has had a change of heart and is now interested in you, or maybe she is boosting her ego by playing with your feelings for her because she is dissatisfied with Mr NBD. There is a saying 'nothing ventured, nothing gained' and if you are still crazy about her then tell her - maybe this is the right time for you both to be together. If she doesn't feel the same way towards you, remember you didn't lose her friendship when she left you ten years ago.*

'You Spend More Time with that Bike than with Me!'
Problems Women Have with Men

Q When we first started going out my boyfriend paid me lots of attention, but then he got 'The Bike!' He assured me that it was for both of us and that we would travel around all over the country. In practise all he does is dismantle it, put it back together again, polish it, and he spends long hours discussing it with his pals. When I went round to see him last night (for what I thought was going to be a romantic dinner for two), he was still in his overalls cleaning the bike. It was the final straw and I snapped 'You spend more time with that bike than with me' and he said I was out of order and unreasonable, and I should be glad he had a bike and not another woman! What do you think?

Sharon, Felixstowe

A *I think that your boyfriend was 'out of order' and unreasonable in not fulfilling his assurances that the bike was for both of you to enjoy travelling around the country, and for not being ready for the romantic dinner that he had promised you. You must understand that everyone needs hobbies, but I feel that his hobby has become as much competition for his time and interest in you as another woman in his life might have been. You must explain to him that in every relationship there must be compromises. He needs to allocate special times to you when you can have his full attention, and special times to his bike, and also time together when you can both enjoy the bike together. If he won't do this, then you should try to find a more considerate boyfriend.*

Q I have been going out with my boyfriend for four years, but we recently had a major row and split up for three months. My boss, who is married, took me out to cheer me up; we got very drunk and landed up in bed together. I have just got back together with my boyfriend but find I am pregnant by my boss! What shall I do?

Julie, Earls Court

A *The first thing you must do is go to have it medically confirmed that you really are pregnant. If you do not want to go to your local GP, you can have a free pregnancy test with the British Pregnancy Advisory Service who will also give you counselling and guidance afterwards on what to do next. If you are pregnant you need to decide as soon as possible whether you want to have the baby and keep it, have it adopted, or have an abortion - there is no time to lose. I strongly recommend you to come clean with your boyfriend - a secret such as this between you could never work. However, don't forget to bear in mind that all this happened whilst you were split up from your boyfriend. Also of course, although you may find it difficult to discuss the subject with him, your boss, the father of your baby, has responsibilities here as well!*

Q I really like a man who works across the road from my office, but I don't know what to do about it. I am rather shy and not at all confident when it comes to relationships. I see him quite often and he is very friendly towards me, and I have been told that he asks his work colleagues about me but says he is too shy to ask me out! I can't ask him out because I am afraid of being rejected. Maybe I should just leave it, but I really like him and want to get to know him better. What do you think?
Jackie, Hastings

A *There is a saying 'Faint heart never won fair man'! Go for it; you've nothing to lose and everything to gain. You like him, and he has indirectly told you via his friends that he likes you too. Although you are afraid of being rejected, I think in this case there is a strong chance you won't be. When you next see him why not ask him if he would like to meet you for a drink and a chat one night after work, and arrange a definite date. Good luck, I hope it goes well for you both.*

Q I've been going out with my boyfriend on and off for 4 years now, and we've had wonderful times together and bad times. All the time I've been with him I've never felt he was committed to our relationship, and have expected him to leave at any time - which he has done frequently. However hard I try to please him, he constantly criticises me or my children, and half the time he accuses me of things that apply to him, not me; he also lives his life in total chaos, although I try my best to organise and clear up after him. I love him dearly but all this has made me feel insecure and nervous, and sometimes I say or do stupid things. Over the last year, although he has not told me, he has driven friends and acquaintances crazy by asking them whether or not he should marry me. We have split up 3 times during this time, and each time he has told me he's off to find the perfect person for him, but he's been back within days or weeks. Over the last month we've been happier

than ever, and he has wanted to spend all his time with me. Yesterday he came round, out of the blue, and calmly told me that we were both getting older, wasting each other's time, and we both needed to go out and look for the perfect person for ourselves, and once again he ended the relationship. I feel in a state of shock and am terrified that he really means it this time. I feel like I have had a limb cut off, and I'm desperate to know is there anything I can do to win him back?
Mandy, Windsor

A *There are some people in this life who are committed to being non-committed. By this I mean that they build up an image of the perfect person they would like to be with that is so unachievable, they will never be able to commit themselves to anyone. Your boyfriend constantly criticises you, and however hard you try to please him, he will find something else to have a go about. This is because from the beginning of any relationship he has to, maybe unconsciously, look for excuses to give him a way out. The fact that he runs away from you when you are at your happiest, is indicative of the fact that he cannot commit himself to a relationship. There is no perfect person out there for any of us - life is full of compromises. I am sure that he does care deeply for you (he would not have been around for so long if he didn't), so that when he is unlucky in his search and misses you, he comes back. What you have to do now is step back and do nothing; counsel yourself as to whether this pattern which he has set, and which could go on for the next 10 years, is what you really want out of life. Do you want to go on feeling insecure, and suffer constant put downs which lessen your feelings of self worth? Unless something dramatic happens to change him, or he has professional help for his problem, I think you are in a 'no go' area. You mustn't blame yourself, you just chose the wrong man!*

Q I was introduced to a brilliant man just over two years ago and it was love at first sight for me. We quickly moved in together and the relationship and friendship between us was fantastic, fun and exciting. Two months ago, quite out of the blue he informed me that he had kissed a female friend of his, and he no longer loved me - in fact he had never loved me! He is now going through a rocky patch in his new relationship and wants to try again with me.

Although I am now in a 'rebound relationship' I still desperately love him and want to see him again, but I couldn't bear to be hurt a second time. He says his feelings for me are genuine and that he made a big mistake in leaving me. Should I try again, or am I just being stupid?
Wendy, Toronto, Canada

A Unfortunately when a man says he doesn't love a woman, he usually means it! I would be very suspicious of a man who suddenly 'out of the blue' says that he doesn't love you, and then a short while later says that he does love you and wants to come back. I would tend to think that he is either very fickle and doesn't know his own mind, or that he is hedging his bets by asking to come back to you, because he knows his new relationship is ending and he doesn't want to be on his own. Either way you may find it difficult to trust him again; it never usually works to take a step backwards. You have survived two months without him; wait and see how you both feel in another two months. Then if you both feel strongly enough about each other, start dating again with a view to total commitment to one another. You must never let anyone mess around with your emotions. If it works out for you, I shall be delighted to have had my doubts proved wrong.

Q I've been seeing Adrian for three years now. He's married with two children aged 10 and 12, and although he still lives with his wife and they share the same bed, there's no relationship left between them. His wife and children know me, but only his wife knows about our relationship. Adrian has always said he can't tell his children about us until they are old enough to understand, and he can't leave home to be with me until then. I have just had Adrian's baby (his family know nothing about her) and I'm finding it more difficult to cope with the situation now, especially since Adrian cannot give me any financial support and his children seem to need him more than ever! He says he loves me very much and that we will be together one day, but now is not the right time to tell his children about us. I love Adrian, I love my baby, but I feel very alone. Help!
Amanda, Truro

A *Adrian certainly seems to be having his cake and eating it! He apparently has a loving wife (she must be to have put up with this situation and still share his bed) and children, and a mistress and new baby he's at liberty to see whenever he wants without any financial or moral responsibilities. No time will ever be the right time to tell his children about you - no matter how old they are they will find it difficult to understand. I'm sorry to be blunt, but I think you have to accept that Adrian does not want to leave his wife and children, and does not want to accept responsibilities for his new family. Please be strong, forget false hopes about this relationship and distance yourself from a man who appears to think only of himself. Seek the help and support of your friends and family, and if possible get professional help from a counsellor. You will find that although life will be painful at first, there's a much brighter future ahead for you if you follow this path.*

Q I met my boyfriend just before Christmas and we've been seeing each other on a regular basis, to the exclusion of my friends. During the first few months he was loving and caring, but now he is not as affectionate as he was. I know he has a heavy work load and is under a lot of pressure, and I try to give support and encouragement which he seems to appreciate, but I feel that the loving, caring man I met 6 months ago has disappeared. I feel very down about it all and would welcome your advice.
Claudine, Lyon, France

A *When two people who are very attracted to each other start going out together, feelings and emotions are at a high pitch. Gradually as the relationship develops and you begin to relax and get to know each other better, these emotions tone down to a lesser degree, especially as day to day living pressures creep in. Your boyfriend is undergoing heavy pressures at work and you are giving him support, but this in turn is giving you pressure as you feel you are getting less love and affection from him than before. You should think a little more about yourself and decide what you want from life. Give him some space to sort out his work pressures, and gain a little independence for yourself by catching up with old friends and doing activities you enjoy. At the same time make sure that the time you spend together is quality time where you can try to bring back some romance into your relationship. You will soon find out whether his feelings for you have changed and it is a situation where 'familiarity breeds contempt', or whether he is truly pre-occupied with work pressures and has forgotten how to show his love and affection for you.*

Q I have been going out with the most perfect man for me for 9 months, and he feels the same way. The problem is that he is married with two young children, and is finding it hard to leave home! I recently met a 55 year old woman at my local health club, who has been a mistress to a married man for 20 years. Her lover always promised he would leave his wife for her, but instead he has just left *her* for a younger mistress of 35. I feel concerned for my future, what shall I do?
Sally, Twickenham

A *Well, if you don't want your situation to be the same in 9 years' time, you had better do something about it soon. I strongly believe in fate, and it was probably a fortuitous day for you when you met this woman! I suggest that you go away for an idyllic few days with your lover, and then without any tears, tell him you are leaving for good. If he really wants to be with you he will, and if he doesn't, the sooner you are away from him the better.*

Q I am 36 years old and lead a hectic life, working erratic hours running a small fashion company as well as bringing up my two children aged 8 and 6, and spending time with my boyfriend Mike. I can manage my job and bringing up my children, but when it comes to household repairs, I just can't cope. Mike has been a tower of strength repairing cupboard doors etc., and in turn I have put myself out to do lots of things for him (which maybe sometimes he doesn't even notice). Recently, although we are still very happy with each other, things are not getting done as they used to be, and I am wondering if he feels that I am taking advantage of him. He also leads a very busy life, and my ex-boyfriend Paul (who I know would like to get back together with me) has offered to help me out. I don't want to offend Mike, what should I do?
Natalie, Sandbach

A *The first thing to do, is ask* him. *Tell him how much you appreciate all the work he has done around your house, and how concerned you are that he might be feeling 'taken advantage of', even though you try to do other things in return for him. Whatever his answer, I don't feel that you should involve Paul. This might well offend Mike, and produce considerable problems with your relationship, to add to your problems with the household repairs. The answer is to employ an odd-job man, and whenever Mike wants to, he can take over again. Above all things, you should never* use *your ex-boyfriend.*

Q I've been single for a few years now, but I started seeing this guy a couple of weeks ago. He seemed to be the perfect match for me, and we got on really well. I'm in my mid thirties and ready to settle down, so I desperately wanted this relationship to work. Last weekend he went out without me, and I phoned him during the evening hoping he would ask me to join him. He didn't, and he wasn't pleased that I had checked up on him. This upset me because I thought, from what he had said previously, that he wanted to be with me all the time. I left an upset message on his answer phone later that night, saying that I didn't like being left on my own. Now he doesn't call me at all, and I am worried that I've blown it with him. I don't want to call him in case he doesn't want to know me any more. Have I frightened him off by being too possessive? I only wanted to be with him, and I don't know what to do now.
Priscilla, I.O.M.

A *First of all, I think you have to take stock of your life, and realise that having a man is not the be all and end all of things. Sometimes when we get to our mid thirties, our biological clock takes over and makes us desperate to find a partner and to settle down. Unfortunately this desperation, although you may not be conscious that you are transmitting it, usually frightens men away. Everyone needs to feel that their partner is a whole person who can cope on their own, who is happy with their own company, has their own interests, and will not only depend on* them *to get their enjoyment from life. This man took one evening off from you, and you threw all your frustrations and wrath at him onto his answer phone. Please try to gain a little independence, and develop some new interests and hobbies of your own. Then phone him up and apologise, and in a light friendly manner ask him if he fancies meeting you for dinner one night. Tell him about all the new things you are starting to do with your life, and see what happens. If he says 'no', at least you know where you stand and can move on, having hopefully learnt from this experience. Never let a man think that being with you will be a life sentence of never being able to do things on his own again!*

Q I am a 25 year old nurse and have been going out with Andy (he's 34) for 18 months. Six months ago he was made redundant, and although he goes for many interviews he can't get a job, and he has been drinking heavily for months. I try my best to help and talk things through with him, but he is getting abusive towards me. He even resents the fact that I'm working and he's on the dole. I love him very much, but the more I love him and do things for him, the worse he is to me. My work is starting to suffer as I am so unhappy, what should I do?
Michelle, Forest Gate

A Andy's male ego will be suffering because he can't get any work, and therefore probably can't afford to take you out or contribute towards any treats. However not everyone who is out of work takes to drink, and you should not excuse his behaviour towards you. If he is not one already, it sounds like Andy is well on the way to becoming an alcoholic, and if you do not step back and refuse to allow yourself to be abused, you will become ill. Alcoholism is like a merry-go-round where all the riders have a part to play in giving the alcoholic an excuse to drink. He will need other excuses beside his lack of work, and you may unwittingly be changed into an unhappy complaining person who will fit the bill. Please step off this merry-go-round before it has time to gain momentum, by walking away from your boyfriend and leaving him to his own devices every time he becomes abusive. Contact Alcoholics Anonymous Family Group (the telephone number is in your local directory) and seek their advice. Whatever happens to this relationship you must put yourself and your work first - it will not benefit either of you if you are both destroyed by the bottle.

QI'm 38 and my boyfriend's 25, and although he's really keen on me and we are really happy together, I feel uneasy. I feel that there's too big an age gap between us and we should break up now, because he'll eventually meet someone more his own age and leave me anyway. He says he doesn't mind about the age difference, and he just loves *me*. Although I love him too, I'm worried that I'm ruining his life; what shall I do?
Vivienne, Leeds

A If I were you, I would just determine to enjoy life with the man you love, who loves you in return. Whatever age gap there could be between you and your boyfriend, he could still meet someone else he preferred at any time and leave you - nothing in this life is certain, so enjoy the present and stop worrying about what might happen in the future. Most of us don't get to chose the person we fall in love with, it just happens. Your boyfriend fell in love with you as a person despite the age gap, and as long as you keep him as happy with you as he is at present, there is less chance that he will leave you for someone else.

'Can You Be a Real Friend?'
Problems Between Friends

QMy friend is always two timing her boyfriend who is one of the nicest guys you could ever hope to meet. I get really upset everytime she tells me what she is getting up to, because I know he is faithful to her and has no idea what is going on. Last night she phoned me and said 'Can you be a real friend and tell John that I was with you last night if he asks'. I don't want to lie to him or be any part of her deceptions, but will she think I'm letting her down as a friend if I don't?
Leanne, Hemel Hempstead

A You must tell your friend the truth that you do not want to get involved. You must tell her how uncomfortable you feel about the whole situation, and that feeling so bad about it you might inadvertently 'let the cat out of the bag'. Your friend will be letting you down as a friend is she insists on making you do something that you do not like!

Q My best friend Jean is getting married and has asked me to be her bridesmaid. Her future husband Geoff has asked his closest friend Derek to be best man. The problem is that I was engaged to Derek last year, and we were planning to marry this summer. We had a terrible row and he broke off the engagement, and we haven't spoken since. I've never stopped loving him, and I don't think I can cope with being so close to him at the altar. Jean tells me that Derek has similar qualms, and has told Geoff he won't be best man if I am the bridesmaid. Geoff and Jean are really upset as they both want their closest friends beside them when they get married. What shall I do?

Mary, Auckland, New Zealand

A *I can imagine how upsetting this situation is for you and Derek, but I do feel that you should both meet and discuss not only the wedding, but the major row that broke your engagement, and see if you can sort your own lives out. Whatever path you choose for yourselves, you need to remember that this is Geoff and Jane's special day. However difficult it may be for you both, try to put on a brave front and place their happiness before your own. I do hope you accept their invitation, and help make it a day they will always treasure.*

Q Rachel and I have been friends since Prep school and have always been close. I recently had to leave my flat, and Rachel let me stay with her and her boyfriend Andrew until I found a new flat. The more time I spent with Andrew, the more I knew that we had something between us, and last week I found myself making love to him in Rachel's bed whilst she was at work. Although Rachel is my best friend, I feel Andrew could be the great love of my life. What should I do?

Tracy, Dunmow

A *Move out at once. Rachel was a good friend to you when you were in difficulties, and you have totally abused her friendship - who needs enemies when they can have a best friend like you! Also, what sort of a man is Andrew to betray his girlfriend in her own bed under her own roof? If he can behave this way to Rachel, you can be assured he would probably do the same to you too! There are certain unwritten rules in this life, and one of them is 'look but never touch a friend's partner or ex-partner'. If you have any loyal feelings left at all for Rachel, you will make sure she never hears about this episode from either of you.*

Q Please help. My best friend Samantha has just told me she has slept with a guy I know called George, and that she is falling in love with him. The problem is that another friend has told me George is bi-sexual. I don't know if it is true or not, so should I tell Samantha?
Kaye, Atlanta

A *Unfortunately you need to have direct proof before you can make allegations about George's sexual behaviour, to Samantha. What you have heard is a rumour, and if it is repeated it could be termed slander. Have talks with Samantha and make sure that she is practising safe sex - emphasise how important this is nowadays as none of us can be sure of our partner's sexual history (even make up a fictitious story about a 'friend' who got herself into tragic difficulties through not following this advice). If you manage to get any definite facts about George that you feel your friend should know about, then tell her immediately.*

Q I recently met a girl at a singles club and we got friendly with each other. She suggested that we both team up and go to a night-club together the next week, and I readily agreed. That night I met a guy I really liked, and at the end of the evening when my friend and I were leaving, he told me his phone number and asked me out for dinner the following weekend. I was really excited and spoke a few times on the phone to my girlfriend during the week deciding what to wear etc. When I met him the following weekend he was a bit strange to start with, and then he told me that my girlfriend had phoned him up the night after we'd been to the night-club, and asked to come over and see him to discuss me with him. When she got to his place she was all over him telling him how much she wanted him, and tried to get him into bed with her. He didn't want to know and eventually she left, but he thought I ought to know about my friend. I was hurt and horrified, and the next day I rang my friend up and asked her to explain herself. She said that all men were fair game and if she liked any man, whether he was with me or with anyone else, she couldn't see why she shouldn't try to get him. She'd done it before, so what was all the fuss about? When she realised I was really upset and didn't want to know her any more, she got hysterical. She begged and pleaded with me not to leave her, and said she was really lonely and didn't have any friends. I feel really bad about the whole thing, and I don't know what to do. What do you think?

Siobhan, Londonderry

A This girl is certainly no friend of yours, and I am not surprised that she has no friends of her own if this is the way she conducts her life. Her behaviour towards you has been appalling, she has shown that she has little respect for your feelings, and you owe it to yourself not to give her the opportunity to do this to you a second time. Explain to her in no uncertain terms why she is once again friendless, and suggest that she goes for counselling sessions to try to sort out her warped way of thinking!

Q I've recently started going out with a gorgeous girl, I see her most nights and we are very happy. My best mate however, keeps telling me that she is no good and will only make me unhappy in the long run, and that I should leave her alone now before I get too fond of her. I used to spend most of my free time with my best mate so he knows me pretty well, could he be right about her?

Darren, Stratford, E. London

A Very often when friends tell us to give up our girlfriends/ boyfriends for whatever reason, they have an ulterior motive for doing so. Your best mate is obviously missing your company and probably has no-one else to go 'hunting' with, therefore it is in his best interests to persuade you give up your girlfriend and be single again. If you are happy in your relationship, that is all that counts. Don't listen to other people, just listen to your own inner feelings and you won't go far wrong. Maybe your girlfriend has single friends she could introduce to your mate? Once your mate has found another playmate, I think the objections to your new relationship will cease!

Q I was devastated when I split up with boyfriend, and now I'm becoming even more upset by the attitudes of some of my friends. They always appeared to like Grant, but instead of offering me sympathy they have passed comments like 'good riddance', and they ask questions like 'have you heard from HIM lately?' with a real tone of disdain as if he were a bad smell under their noses. I feel confused and hurt. They know I still love Grant so why should they be bad-mouthing him now? Why did they never tell me before that they disliked him? Now he has started phoning me again and I actually feel scared to tell my friends I might go back to him - they've made me feel almost ashamed of him. How can I avoid falling out with my friends?
Kim, Basingstoke

A *Maybe your friends know something about Grant and the break-up of your relationship that they haven't told you about, and feel concerned for your welfare. Talk to your friends about how you are feeling and ask them if there is anything detrimental that they know about Grant which they are keeping from you. Tell them that if there is something, it is vitally important for you to know (however painful it may be for you to hear) because he has started phoning you again and you are thinking of going back to him - but although you love him you don't want to get hurt again, and you need their reassurance that you would be doing the right thing. Listen to what they have to say as dispassionately as you can, go away and think about, and then make up your own mind. At the end of the day it doesn't matter what other people think of Grant, because if you love him and want to be with him that is all that counts; you are responsible for your own destiny.*

Q I became friends with Susan because she was going out with my boyfriend's mate Pete. When Susan and Pete split up, my boyfriend Bruce and I still kept in touch with both of them. Recently I split up with Bruce and Pete was really kind to me; he phoned me up lots, and he took me out to dinner to cheer me up. But then he started 'trying it on' with me and I got really upset. I'd always thought of him as 'a mate' and now I think he thinks I've led him on in some way. But how could he think this as he knows Susan's my friend,

and he's supposed to be Bruce's friend? He even hinted that he thought *they* were now seeing each other. I don't want to lose his friendship, but I'm afraid I've got caught up in some strange revenge game against Susan. What should I do?
Sandie, Perth, W. Australia

A *Just be honest with Pete and tell him how much his help and sympathy meant to you, and how much you value his friendship, but that is as far as it goes. Tell him much you would miss his friendship if he decides that this is not enough for him, but there is no point in the two of you starting a relationship, just because Bruce and Susan may be seeing each other, if you do not feel the same way about him. For your own sake change your social scene and try to break away from this foursome, and cultivate new friends. Join a local sports club or gym, or join a reputable singles club which has a large membership and a proven track record. It's now time to move forward, and leave those in the past to play whatever games they may wish to make them happy.*

LIVING TOGETHER

'How Much Longer Are You Going To Be in The Bathroom?'
Problems Men Have with Partner/Spouse

Q I live with my lady friend in the country each weekend, although we are apart during the week because I work in town. I really look forward to seeing her, but nearly every week we finish the weekend in a blazing row because on Monday mornings she always takes ages in the bathroom and makes me late for work. When I ask her how much longer she is going to be in the bathroom, she never seems to hear and I get hopping mad. She always looks wonderful, without having to spend hours doing her hair and plastering on her make-up and I've told her this but it makes no difference. I put up with her hogging the bathroom during the weekend, but how can I make her understand that on Monday morning my getting to work on time is more important than her vanity?
Jeremy, London W.1.

A *Why don't you get up extra early and bring her breakfast in bed. She will be amazed and delighted, and while she is enjoying her treat, you can hog the bathroom!*

Q I am 33, and have been living with Jane (aged 37) for five years. She has a daughter from a previous marriage, and we all get on well together. I want to marry her, but she says she never wants to marry again. She also doesn't want to have any more children, and wants me to have a vasectomy. I love them both, but I am not sure that I want this operation. What's your advice?
'Worried', Utah, U.S.A.

A *Things seem to be a little one sided here. Jane doesn't want to tie the marriage knot, but she expects one to be tied for you! If she does not want any more children, and is not prepared to commit herself in marriage to you, why not suggest that she could consider having a sterilisation operation. You can never know what life has in store for*

you, and if this relationship should end, you are far too young at the age
of 33 to deny yourself and a future partner the opportunity to have
children of your own.

Q Carolyn and I have known each other for a year now.
She is divorced with two children with whom I get on very
well, and three months ago we all moved into a flat together. We are
planning to get married next year and I am so in love with her, but
I am also terrified of losing her. I have a good job, and as she has no
money at all of her own I support all three of them, as well as
supporting my ex-wife and our children. The problem is that Carolyn
is not satisfied with our life-style, and is forever openly complaining
to me and to our friends that we don't have enough money to do all
the things she wants to do. She has tried going for job interviews
but always finds excuses as to why the job is not right for her, and
she has even started blaming me for not finding her the perfect job.
I give her as much as I can, and I have just bought a new car to please
her, but now she is threatening to leave to find someone else who
can give her more. I am doing my best but the loan repayments on
this flat are crippling, and my health is suffering. I really adore her,
so what should I do?
Warren, Philadelphia, U.S.A.

A *There is a saying that 'love is blind', and in this instance*
I think it is true! Does your girlfriend really want you, or does she
want what she thinks you should be providing for her? You are not
married, yet you have acquired a 'nagging wife' and your health is
suffering. You have to be strong and tell her that you are doing the best
you can, but if this is not good enough for her and is making her unhappy,
maybe she should look elsewhere. You may well find that her attitude
rapidly changes when she realises she could lose you! You must have
some serious discussions as to what you both want and need from life,
and also think long and hard about your plans to marry next year.

Q I am 40 years old and married, but I don't love my wife
any more. She has funded everything we own from her trust
fund, and we lead a very comfortable life. We have two children and
I love them very much, but I have fallen in love with my 25 year old
secretary at work. Do I stay with my wife and enjoy the comfort of

her money, or should I leave and move into my secretary's one bedroom flat?
Peter, Walsall

A *I think there is far more at stake here than just losing a comfortable life-style with your wife. The most important people in this scenario are your children, and I think you should discuss the situation with your wife and a marriage guidance counsellor as soon as possible to see if there is any way in which you can save your marriage. Any marriage will become stale and boring if you both don't work hard at keeping up the romance and interest in each other, and the grass will always seem greener on the other side. However no one is perfect, and after a few years you will find that exactly the same problems and boring routines which you are experiencing now will crop up in your new relationship, and you may well start searching for a new more exciting partner again. You say that you are in love with your secretary, but please make sure that you are not risking your marriage and the happiness of your children for an unrealistic dream. You also need to bear in mind that helpful and obedient secretaries do not necessarily make helpful and obedient wives!*

Q My wife is still a very attractive woman facially, and she has a cupboard full of beautiful clothes, most of which I bought for her. The problem is that since the birth of our last child three years ago, she has let herself go and these clothes no longer fit her. In fact she now looks and dresses like a frump to hide her figure. Whilst my love for her goes deeper than her appearance, it still upsets me that she no longer seems to care for herself or the way she looks. Please advise.
Russ, Leicester

A *Many women put on a lot of excess weight during pregnancy for various reasons, and once they have given birth they are often too busy and exhausted to discipline their eating habits and they eat even more. Instead of regaining their pre-pregnant shape, the weight starts to pile on and they try to disguise what is happening to their figure by wearing shapeless clothes. Your wife is probably just as discontented as you are with the way she looks, and she really needs your help and understanding. Why don't you make arrangements for the children to be looked after for a week, and take her off to a health farm. You can both relax, de-stress and exercise, and it will be easier there for her to be helped to change her eating habits. You might also suggest that you both join a gym together to work off the excess pounds. Give her lots of encouragement and praise as the pounds roll off, and you'll be amazed how quickly your wife will start to take an interest in her appearance again.*

Q Over the last few years my wife has become a high-powered business executive and has started to earn a great deal more than I do. I feel very inferior, although my wife tells me not to be so stupid as she does not feel superior to me. I feel she is starting to lose her patience with me, but how can I cope with the way I feel?
Alan, Brighton

A Stop feeling sorry for yourself and start feeling proud of your wife and her achievements. Don't bring your wife down through your own self pity when it is obviously completely unnecessary, and be aware that if you make her too unhappy she may leave you. Please stop moaning and be grateful for, and enjoy what you have.

Q I suspect that my wife talks about our relationship with her women friends. Whatever little tiff we have, I'm sure it is dissected over and over again between them, and I really dislike this. I feel uncomfortable that so many people know so much about me, and it undermines the privacy of our relationship. What should I do?
Dennis, Purley

A You need to tell her in the nicest possible way that you are well aware of what is going on, and that you don't like it and would prefer her not to. You also have to be aware that this is one of the fundamental differences between men and women, in that women feel the need to discuss their problems endlessly with their friends, and men tend to retreat into their shells and go quiet. Tell her that she must feel free to voice her doubts to you about any problem you may have in your relationship, so that you and she can sort it out together, and then there will be no need for her to discuss it with her friends.

QI don't know what's happening to me. I'm a 45 year old male with a wonderful wife, children that any man could be proud of, a beautiful home, a successful business which provides me with more than enough money, but I'm screaming inside my head! I should be the happiest man alive but I keep thinking there must be more to life than this. Why do young women seem so attractive to me now? I feel distant from my wife, and although I know I'm causing her a lot of pain I just can't help myself. Should I leave home now before I destroy us all?
Angus, Dunfermline

A It sounds like you are going through what is commonly known as the male menopause. Take heart, most men go through this, and the majority of them come through unscathed and a little wiser. Try to cultivate as many new hobbies and interests (especially sport) as you can, take your wife away on holiday to try to rekindle your interest in her, and seek counselling help as soon as possible to sort out your emotional difficulties.

QMy wife and I have dreadful rows, and often they are over very trivial things. We both have quick tempers and we seem to fall into these screaming matches far too easily. We are devoted to each other and get on really well when we're not fighting. I hate being at odds with her but I can't seem to stop myself. How can we prevent these rows from starting?
Bob, Detroit, U.S.A.

A Most of us tend to hurt the ones we love the most, and only have screaming matches with those we feel comfortable enough to be able to do so - and it is often good to clear the air. However this can get out of hand with the arguments taking over the good times, which in the long run will be detrimental to your relationship. Therefore you both need to learn to control your tempers and be more tolerant of each other - and grow up. Whenever you feel your temper rising, take a deep breath, stop and think, and walk away from a potentially explosive situation.

'Your Dinner's in The Dog!'
Problems Women Have
with Partner/Spouse

QSince my boyfriend moved in I have had a real problem. I ask him to phone me if he's going to be late home from work so that I know what to do about dinner. He never does, and when he eventually gets home we have an argument. He says I am trying to control him and that he shouldn't have to report to me all the time. He says I should just go ahead and eat by myself if he's late, but I prefer to wait and eat with him if he's due home; I think one of the pleasures of living together is shared mealtimes. Often I end up eating a stewed dinner alone, and give his dinner to the dog. When I tell him his dinner's in the dog he gets angry! I think he's being really selfish but he doesn't see it that way at all, and he says I'm trying to play married instead of living together. Am I being unreasonable?
Debbie, Croydon

A*No you're not being unreasonable, but maybe you both have different ideas as to the nature of your relationship. I think that you should call your boyfriend's bluff and get out a little more and develop some other interests. If he just wants to behave like a flat-mate, then cook for yourself when you feel hungry, and only arrange to eat together when it is mutually convenient to you both. He will start to appreciate you more if he ceases to feel he is being pushed into something he doesn't want. Hopefully you will both enjoy each others company more, or maybe you will decide that this is not the sort of relationship you were seeking!*

QMy partner is an Aries male aged 34, and I am an Aries female aged 29. He was living with me and my 7 year old daughter for over a year when things went wrong; we agreed to have a break but still met every weekend. This went on for 2 months and he was still unsure of what he wanted out of life, so I told him I wanted to end the relationship. He agreed, but the following day he came back begging me to give him another chance. I did because I really love him, and so he returned to live with us and we planned to marry this September. Then we had a disagreement about the flat

he had bought whilst we were apart, and he just left again. He says he loves me and regrets leaving, but he still doesn't know what he wants and is afraid of commitment. I am really confused. He seems to contradict himself. What do you think? Will it ever work out? I look forward to your reply.
Joy, Dorking

A If you continue to let him walk all over you, by moving in and out of your life as he pleases, I have serious doubts that this relationship will ever work out. You are quite right that he seems to contradict himself, and he in turn is right when he says he is afraid of commitment. The most important person in this equation is your 7 year old daughter, and if life continues in this pattern, she will become more emotionally screwed up than either of you. For all your sakes, I advise you to end this relationship, and mean it. *Your partner will be forced into making a decision, and if he decides he cannot live without you and your daughter, and is prepared to commit himself, then Good Luck to you all. If he still dithers and doesn't know what he wants, he may* never *know what he wants, and you are well out of it. You will have saved yourself many valuable years of heartache. At 29, you still have years ahead of you to find someone who knows he really wants* you.

Q Although we both originate from New Zealand, I met my husband in London (I am 38 and he is 33). He really wanted to stay in England, and as I already had a British Passport we married sooner than we might have done in different circumstances. I made it very clear from the beginning that I would eventually like to have children and then move back to New Zealand to bring them up, and he agreed to this. We have been married for five years now, and I really want to have a child and move back to New Zealand, but my husband won't go back and says he doesn't want children yet. I feel devastated! He has a good job here, but I know he could get a comparable one back in New Zealand. I also know that if I went back to New Zealand I could get a good job. The situation between us has got really bad, and we bicker and argue all the time. We are not sure now whether we even love each other enough to stay together. Do you think the age gap between us has anything to do with this? What should I do?
Barbara, Kensington

A At the age of 38 you are bound to feel more urgency than your husband about starting a family now, because your biological clock is working overtime telling you that it is time to do so. Although with modern obstetrics many women are able to have their first child in their forties with safety, you need to establish as soon as possible whether or not your husband definitely wants to have children with you, and if so when. If he says he doesn't know, or is vague about when he would like to have them, I think you should discuss whether you both still share the same dreams and can go forward together to try to make them come true, or whether you have grown apart and feel it might be better for both of you to part and start afresh. It is better for you to find out his true intentions now, rather than find out later when it might be too late to have children with someone else in the country in which you would like to live.

Q My husband has just been made redundant at the age of 50. Although he received enough compensation for us not to be in financial difficulties, he is very depressed and seems to have lost his motivation to do anything. There is so much he could do now that he has the time, there are so many ambitions to fulfil, but his inability to get another job has made him give up on life. He had always looked forward to retirement, but now he feels he has been thrown on the scrap heap. How can I help him?
Judith, Southend

A Your husband feels he is a failure and needs help to restore his faith in his abilities. Try to get him to visit his GP to see if he needs medical help with his depression, and suggest that he also makes an appointment to see a careers advisor. He needs to be motivated to feel that losing his job is not the end of his career, but could be the start of a new exciting one in a field he has never even considered before. Many people today have to change tack around his age because of redundancy, and he may find that this could give him a new lease of life and a sense of purpose if he goes along with it. He has received enough financial compensation not to have to worry too much about what his new occupation will pay, and he has everything to gain from a rewarding change of scene. Try to convince him that this could be the luckiest break of his life so far.

Q I love the man I live with very much, but what I am finding very difficult is his constant criticisms of me and everyone else he knows, and his frequent attempts to try to change me into his ideal 'perfect' woman! He doesn't seem to have a good word to say about anyone, and I know he grumbles about me behind my back to all our friends. I feel under constant pressure to please him all the time and to change to whatever he wishes me to be. He can be so loveable, carefree and friendly, but then this darker side takes over. What do I do?

Carole, Windsor

A Your man seems to have a really bad problem - himself! If he always criticises and grumbles about everyone else, then the problem must surely lie within him. He may well feel inadequate, and that is why, when things go wrong in his life, he has to pull everyone down around him and criticise them - which in his eyes will seem to raise himself above them. Also because deep down inside himself he knows he is less than perfect, he has to try to make others around him 'perfect' in the hope that it will rub off on him! You can try to build up his confidence and help him, but above all you must explain how hurtful it is to have him criticise you to your friends, and that any problems you have should be dealt with between the two of you. No one is perfect, and if he continues to try to change you, you will not be the person he was originally attracted to, and he may lose your love and you!

Q I was madly in love with Peter, and last week we got married. During the wedding reception Peter disappeared for half an hour, and I went to look for him. The reception was in a large hotel, and as I walked into an 'empty' banqueting suite I found him in a compromising situation with his best man! He never told me he was gay, and I have not felt able to let him touch me since. My whole world has been shattered. He says he loves me, but he also needs the affection of men as well. I still love him but I don't think I can handle all this, and I don't think I can live with him. I feel desperate, please help.

Vicky, Maidenhead

A Of course you don't feel able to cope with this situation - few people could. Peter has behaved outrageously towards you, because not only has he betrayed your loving trust in him, he may well have put your health at risk! From what you tell me, you have not consummated your marriage and can therefore go to the courts to have the marriage annulled. I cannot say that this will be an easy period in your life, but time is a great healer and it may be best that you leave home and start this healing process as soon as possible! Accept help and support from friends and family, and if necessary contact your nearest branch of Relate for professional counselling. You have been courageous enough to ask for help, so please take the next step forward to a much brighter future just waiting out there for you.

Q I've been living with my boyfriend for a year, and last month he had to go away on a business trip for four nights. While he was away his brother, who I have always found attractive, phoned and said he was in London and could he stay for a couple of nights. I had to say 'yes', and on the second night of his stay we went out for dinner and landed up in bed together. The next day I felt really guilty, and we agreed that we did not want a relationship with each other, we would never let it happen again, and that we would never tell my boyfriend what had happened. I thought the whole episode was over, but it's just been confirmed that I'm pregnant and I'm not sure who the father is! My boyfriend is over the moon and insists that we get married as soon as possible. I love him very much, but how can I marry him when I could be deceiving him as to the parenthood of my child?
Justine, Esher

A *Normally I would always advocate that 'honesty is the best policy', but in this situation I feel that it would be better for all your sakes, to keep quiet and get on with making the rest of your life a success. If you take this route, you must be strong and never voice your fears about who your baby's real father could be to anyone, however tempted you may feel to do so. If you decide to unburden your fears to your boyfriend, you risk causing a rift between the two brothers, you risk losing a loving father for your baby, and you already know that you and your boyfriend's brother do not want to be committed to each other. Your boyfriend is 'over the moon'; he wants to marry you and you love him - two loving and caring parents is the best start in life you could possibly give to your baby.*

Q We've been married for 22 years and our youngest daughter has just gone to University. My husband has suddenly announced that now all the children are off our hands, he doesn't want me sitting around doing nothing and twiddling my thumbs! He says why should he still have to work hard and have the financial burden of the children, whilst I don't contribute a penny and live a life of luxury and idleness! He feels that I should have an equal share of the financial burden, but I haven't been out to work for 17 years! He's adamant in his views, and I just don't know what to do. Please tell me.

Angela, Chalfont St Peter

A Do you really need the money, or is he just jealous of your new freedom? Whatever the reason calm down, stop worrying and decide what you would like to do with your life now. I am sure you have worked hard all your married life bringing up your children and looking after your husband and your home, and you probably feel like having a bit of a rest. However having led such an active life you may get bored with having less to do, and it might be a good idea to explore the prospect of finding a part-time job to capture your interest, earn some extra money, and meet other people. If you gain a little independence you will have more things to talk about with your husband, and the extra money will make him feel less of a 'meal ticket'. Of course the busier you become, the more he may have to help you with looking after the house, which might be something that he has not yet considered! Talk to a careers advisory officer about what you could do, and see what local classes are available to develop your talents and to learn new skills. Life is one long learning process which only stops on the day we die. Grab hold of any opportunity that is offered to you - this could be an exciting new chapter in your life.

Q I'm married to a TV 'Sportsaholic'! My husband wants to watch every sport you could imagine on television all the time, and invariably falls asleep during the programme. I can't bear watching sport, and as soon as he's nodded off I switch channels. However, I only ever manage to watch about 5 minutes of my favourite programmes before he wakes up and angrily switches the channel back again. I am going out of my mind with boredom, and our relationship is suffering because of it. What shall I do?

Pauline, Newcastle

A Get a second television, and then you can both watch
whatever programme you like! Seriously though, is there not more
to life than just watching the 'box'? What has gone wrong with your
relationship that has made you both lose the art of conversing with each
other, and generally going out and enjoying yourselves? I think you need
to address the problem with your husband as soon as possible, and if you
find it too difficult to sort matters out between the two of you, seek the
help of a third party in some counselling sessions before you bore each
other to distraction!

'Now Take My Mother-in-Law - Please?'
Problems with the 'In-Laws'

Q I have two children from my previous marriage, and I
am engaged to be married in three months time to Paul who I
live with. I would be the happiest girl in the world if it were not for
one big problem - my future mother-in-law! Paul adores her and
has always been heavily influenced by anything she says, and I have
been able to live with this up till now. Her interference in our
relationship is becoming intolerable as she criticises my children
and tells *him* how they should be brought up, she tells him what
decorations and furnishings we should have in the new house we are
moving to, and has told him who we *can't* have to our wedding!
This is causing rows between Paul and I, because he says I am being
unreasonable and she is only trying to help. I am getting upset because
he is taking onboard everything she says, and not listening to any of
my wishes at all. I really feel like calling the whole thing off, and
moving out. I can take most things, but I wish someone would take
my mother-in-law - Please?
Elaine, Romford

A I do not think that you are being unreasonable in objecting
to a third party trying to come between you, your children and
your future husband, however well meaning they may be. Sit down with
Peter and gently but firmly explain that he either has to break away
from his mother's apron strings and think for himself, or face the prospect

of losing you. You want to marry him, not his mother, and you are about to embark on a partnership agreement in which both of you must have an equal say and feel happy about it. You are happy to be welcoming and friendly to his mother, but are not prepared to have your lives run by her. He has to grow up and accept responsibility for himself and his new family, or stay single and be responsible to his mother. He has everything to gain if he makes the former decision, and if he does I am sure he will not lose his mother's love but he might win her respect.

Q My partner dislikes my parents to such an extent that I feel embarrassed to invite them round to visit us, or even to arrange to meet them anywhere with her. She refuses to come with me when I go to visit them and I know they are hurt by the situation. They always ask after her, should I ask her to make more of an effort?
Alastair, Oxford

A Yes you should, and ask her to do it as a favour to you. If your partner cared enough for you she would want to be pleasant to your family and friends, for your sake. Also any adult should be able to be polite to others for a couple of hours at least. What will happen if you have children one day and their grandparents want to visit them, or want to invite you as a family to stay with them?

Q My in-laws are becoming overbearing. Dave's Mumcomes round twice a week and does the housework, washing etc. like she used to when Dave got divorced. At first I thought 'this is handy' but now it's getting on my nerves - I don't *want* her washing our 'smalls'. His Dad is planning to redecorate our house again - he means well, but he is taking over. One day last week he arrived unannounced at 8am (on his way to work) to get us to pick flooring from a brochure. He's just like the Harry Enfield 'Only Me' character on telly. All this is made worse by the fact that they both have keys to the house. Our first baby is due next month and it already has clothes and toys up to the age of five (courtesy of the in-laws). I feel like a coiled spring - any day now I'm sure I will blow a gasket and be really rude to Dave's parents - either that, or have a terrible row with Dave. He says I'm just suffering from hormonal moodiness. Am I right to want some 'space' of my own?
Lorraine, Greenwich

A Try not to blow a gasket, but tell your in-laws clearly and firmly that you need privacy in your own home. You also need plenty of rest and a stress free life before the birth of your baby, and although you appreciate their help you will let them know when you want it. You also need to be given notice of any visits in future in case it is inconvenient to you; they have your house keys but you would appreciate it if they only used them when requested to by you or Dave. You and Dave will have your own child next month, and must be given the privilege of making your own decisions about the baby. Dave must also be made to understand that what was acceptable for him as a single man, must change now that he has a wife and child. If you get too stressed and cannot get through to them all, enlist the help of your doctor or social worker who are there for your well being, especially at this important time in your pregnancy.

Q Now that my in-laws are getting older, my mother-in-law is getting very short tempered with my father-in-law. She speaks harshly to him and puts him down at every available opportunity. She doesn't realise she's doing this and how her behaviour affects him, but I can see that he is crushed and hurt by her sarcastic comments. I've tried talking to my husband about all this but he just wants to keep out of it. He points out to me that she is not a well person, and that she suffers a lot of pain from her arthritis. I realise all this and I feel sympathy for her, but how can I make her understand the pain she is causing her husband?
Catherine, Durban, S.Africa

A There may be many reasons why your mother-in-law behaves as she does towards her husband. The pain she is suffering may well make her short tempered and liable to lash out to those closest to her, but she may just be irritated and fed up with her husband. Have a private word with your father-in-law to ascertain whether or not he is getting as upset as you think he is. I am sure that he realises how much pain she is going through, although he may not understand that this is the reason why she behaves as she does towards him. Let him know that he has everyone's support and sympathy, and encourage him to stand up for himself. Also suggest that he sees more of his friends, and involves himself with outside hobbies and activities if he can. If he spends more time apart from her he will gain strength and have less opportunity to get hurt by her verbal violence, and she *might even miss him and begin to appreciate his company.*

Q I recently got married, and although my in-laws seemed fairly reasonable people before I put the ring on my wife's finger, I now realise I have married into a bizarre scene - in fact I have nicknamed her family 'The Mafia'! Her family have to approve everything we do. If we decide to buy a new piece of furniture, go away for the weekend, or have a dinner party, the news races round the family grapevine. People whose opinions I wouldn't normally dream of seeking (members of her family), give me their opinions about everything and anything we do, and expect me to listen and obey. My wife seems to be completely under their thumb, and is a different girl to the one I married. I can't stand it, please help!
Terry, Walthamstow

A *Are you a man or a mouse? Put your foot down and tell your wife that you married her, not her family. If you are going to have a future together, you have to decide between the two of you what you want out of life, and not listen to others. If she truly loves you and wishes to remain your partner, she will support you and respect your wishes. Have you thought of moving away from the family - maybe to Australia?*

Q My husband hates his father and step-mother, but isn't brave enough to tell them not to come and visit us. They live abroad, and when they come to see us they stay for two weeks at a time. While they are with us my husband is rude to them, and short-tempered with me and the children. I have to do all the running around for them, but he does nothing. It's intolerable and I wish they wouldn't stay, but I realise that they need to see their grandchildren. They know he hates their visits, and all the time they are here, they wind him up! What is the solution?
Eleanor, Inverness

A *The next time they wish to come and stay, tell them that you think that it would be better for all of you (considering the way previous visits have worked out) if they stay at a local hotel or guest house - if they can't afford it your husband should help toward the cost, if only for the peace it will afford him!. If they can visit your home for set periods of time, maybe your husband can grow up and be pleasant to them within these time limits for your sake as well as the children's. Also*

*they could take their grandchildren out for treats by themselves, and
sometimes your husband could be out at business meetings etc. when
they come to visit. It's tough on you, but you are right - they deserve to
see their grandchildren, and it would be churlish to deny them this
pleasure.*

Q I have been living with my partner for a few months,
despite her parents' disapproval, and we now want to get
married. Our problem is that she is Jewish and I am not, and her
parents are putting pressure on me to convert to Judaism. I am not
all that bothered, but I know that my family would be very upset if
our future children were not brought up in the Christian faith. What
should we do?
Duncan, London

A *You must both go and talk to your Priest and her Rabbi.
You will find that the Rabbi is not after converts, and will tell you
that it is wrong to convert for marriage only, and you should only do so
if you truly believe in the Jewish faith. In this country it is usual for
children to take their father's nationality and their mother's religion.
Although your future children would take their mother's religion, you
could both bring them up as humanists - caring human beings who do
not practise any particular religion. Then when your children are old
enough, they could decide for themselves which faith they would prefer
to follow. Eventually both sets of parents I am sure would accept the
situation, but I do think you should both take a little time now to decide
what you really want, and don't just marry in haste. If you do decide to
get married and neither of you converts to the other religion, you will of
course have to have a civil wedding.*

'You Treat This Place Like a Bloody Hotel!'
Problems Parents Have with Children

Q We have a teenage son of 19 and he's driving us to distraction. When he's in, he just loafs around watching the TV or spends hours on the telephone talking to his friends. He never lifts a finger to help me in the house, and his bedroom looks like a hovel. He expects his food to be ready and waiting for him whenever he requests it, and leaves dirty cups and dishes around the house after he's made himself a snack. He comes in at all hours, waking us up as he stumbles up to bed, and his father (who is usually a fairly mild-tempered man) was moved to shout at him at 3am this morning 'You treat this place like a bloody hotel!' He's become insolent and uncommunicative, and we don't know how much longer we can put up with his unreasonable behaviour. What should we do?
Joyce, Guildford

A Many teenagers go through difficult behavioural problems, but your son is almost out of his teens and needs to grow up and behave like a responsible adult. You need to talk to your son and set down some house rules for all your sakes. He has to understand that sharing a home is a matter of team work, and if he can't show consideration for the rest of the family, he can't expect them to show some for him. If he doesn't toe the line don't cook for him, don't clean up after him, don't do his washing and ironing, install a pay-phone, and tell him that he must get home at a reasonable time and not wake you up, or you will lock the front door! If he cannot accept these rules, he may need to consider sharing a flat with a friend where he can drive them crazy instead!

Q We have a little girl aged 4, and I have just given birth to a baby boy. We would be a very happy family except for one thing, my little girl is extremely jealous of her baby brother and I am frightened of leaving them alone in the same room together. I left them together for a couple of minutes yesterday whilst I went to answer the doorbell, and when I came back the baby was screaming

as my daughter had bitten his arm. Although my husband says I am over-reacting, I feel very concerned about the situation and would like to know how to deal with it.
Darlene, Cork

A If your baby boy is receiving more attention than your little girl from you, your husband and visitors, she will be feeling hurt and left out and will do anything to attract your attention - even hurt the baby. Try not to convey your anxiety to your daughter, and show her more love and attention than ever, and when you have visitors ask them to do the same. Each time the baby is bought a present, try to give your little girl a treat as well. Try to involve her as much as possible in looking after the baby with you, letting her know how much he needs her and how much you appreciate her help, and make her feel important. Tell her that time passes quickly, and it won't be too long before he is running around and can be her playmate.

Q My daughter was always very bright at school, and she excelled in her work as well as being captain of the hockey team. At the age of 16 she moved to a co-ed college and met Jeff (who wasn't very bright) and fell in love with him. Her work deteriorated as it seemed she did not want to do better in her exams than him. I sent her off to St Lucia for 6 months to try to get him out of her mind, but eventually she came back, started living with him and got pregnant. As they had no money and he was unemployed I regularly gave her substantial cheques, and 3 years later they decided to get married. I had recently given her another large cheque (which I really couldn't afford) as they were very much in debt, when she told me they were off to have a honeymoon of a life-time in South Africa. I noticed all the new hi-fi equipment they had just bought themselves, and I told her a few home truths about finances and personal responsibilities. She never spoke to me again and banned me from the wedding ceremony. Four months later Jeff found letters which confirmed she'd had an affair in St Lucia whilst they were apart, and he has given her grief about it ever since. She has just been offered a wonderful job in St Lucia and wants to go back with her daughter, but Jeff says he will not be able to get any work over there

and does not want to go. Their marriage is falling apart and I am concerned for my daughter. What can I do?
Austin, Salisbury

A *First of all, I think you need to make contact with your daughter who really needs you now. Try to patch things up between you, even if it means biting your tongue and apologising for the harsh words you must have said to her just before she got married. It sounds to me as if your daughter wants to end her marriage, and sees the job in St Lucia as an opportunity to break away from Jeff. She needs all the love and unbiased support you can give her now, to get through this difficult period in her life. Explain your financial position in that you cannot afford to financially support her indefinitely, at the same time letting her know that whatever she decides to do, you will always be there for her.*

Q I have a beautiful and talented 14 year old daughter. Last week I was cleaning out her room when I found a packet of condoms, and although the packet was still full it had been opened. I have always encouraged my children (aged 14, 12, and 9) to be open with me and with each other, and I can't bear the thought that my daughter is having underage sex, especially without discussing it with me. She is very headstrong, and I don't know how to confront the situation. Please advise.
Linda, Peterborough

A *I can understand your dilemma and how worried you must be, but maybe you are jumping to certain conclusions too soon. Engineer a time when you can be completely on your own with your daughter, and can talk freely as friends about everything. Eventually mention that you found the condoms in her room and see what she says. If they were bought as a joke by her or a friend, then move quickly on to another topic. If she is contemplating having, or is having sex with a boyfriend, praise her for being sensible enough to want to have 'safe sex'. However point out that she is legally underage, and will be putting her boyfriend at risk of getting into considerable problems with the law if they are found out. Stress that if they really care for each other, neither one should want to get the other into serious trouble. Also tell her that*

*she should only ever consider having sex with someone she really cares
for, and who she knows really cares for her.*

Q I have a teenage daughter who resents me because she
feels that I do not have enough time for her. I work 9-5 to
support us, and am currently attending college at night so that I can
provide us with a better life. What shall I do so she doesn't feel
neglected?
Lotte, Copenhagen, Denmark

*A Maybe to your daughter, providing a better life means
spending some time with her mother. If you continue as you are
you may reap the monetary rewards later, but then find that your
daughter has felt so neglected that she is no longer around to share them
with you! You need to explain to her that you are working so hard for
the benefit of both of you, and that you miss her too. Your 9-5 job is a
necessity you cannot change, but maybe you could cut out a couple of
college evenings each week and devote these to your daughter. On the
evenings you have to work, discuss with her as to whether she would like
to have a friend or relative round, or maybe she could develop a hobby
so that she does not have time to feel lonely and miss you so much. You
could even teach her how to cook, so that on some of these evenings she
might prepare a tasty meal you could enjoy together on your return. If
you show as much interest as possible in her life, and encourage her to
develop her own interests, life will soon become easier for you both and
she will feel less neglected.*

Q I am 29 and an only son living at home with my mother.
I would have left home ages ago, but my father died in an accident
five years ago and my mother has become more and more dependent
on me. I have tried bringing girlfriends home to meet her but none of
them have ever been good enough for her, and at times she has been
openly hostile. I recently met a wonderful girl and we have been seeing
a lot of each other, unbeknown to my mother. Although I want to, I
am reluctant to introduce her to my mother as I feel this relationship is
very special, and I don't want anything to spoil it. What should I do?
John, Coventry

A There is a saying 'A coward dies a thousand deaths, a brave man only once!' Take your courage in both hands and face your mother with the problem. Tell her that this girl is very special in your life, and therefore it is important to you that your mother accepts the situation with good grace. Assure her that she will never lose your love for her as a son, and although she may feel threatened that your girlfriend might take you away from her and she will 'lose' her son, she might gain a daughter instead! You have done your best to be loyal and supportive to her for many years, and now it is time to take charge of your own life with hopefully some support from your mother. If she cannot accept the situation you should consider moving out, and you may find that this move could be the making of a much better relationship with both your mother and your new girlfriend.

Q I am very concerned about my 23 year old daughter Sue and her boyfriend Tim. Tim thinks the world of Sue, centres his activities around her, and would do anything for her. However, when I took them both out to dinner last week I was very upset by the way she talked so sharply to him, and behaved in such an uncaring way towards him. I phoned Tim today and asked how things were going, and he admitted that Sue was being increasingly more unpleasant to him and how hurt her behaviour made him feel. He has tried to talk to Sue, but she won't discuss their problems at all and just loses her temper with him. He has asked for my advice; what shall I tell him?
William, New England, U.S.A.

A Sometimes when people are too nice to us we get bored, and we treat them badly in order to provoke a reaction which might hopefully recapture our initial interest in them. Sometimes when a person wants to end a relationship, they do not have the courage to say what they feel. They will behave so badly to their partner that in the end the partner will also become disillusioned and end the relationship. This is an ideal way for someone who likes to appear to be a victim, to end a relationship! I don't know what is going on in Sue's mind, but I do feel that Tim should withdraw a little and become more independent from Sue. I don't mean that he should see other women, but I suggest that he should be less tolerant of Sue's behaviour and embark on some leisure pursuits such as golf, the gym, squash etc. on his own or with his friends. This change in character will either shock Sue into realising how much *she wants him and make her change her attitude towards him, or if she no longer wants him, it will make the break-up of their relationship easier as Tim starts to make an independent life of his own. Whatever happens, I think they are both very lucky to have such a caring parent as you to want to help them through their difficulties.*

Q My little boy aged 3 can be really naughty, and he always manages to push my buttons. Sometimes I feel I'm only one step away from doing him harm. My voice is hoarse with shouting, and I'm ashamed of myself. I love him dearly but half the time I could kill him! How can I prevent a tragedy?
Erica, Oslo, Norway

A *Go to your doctor immediately and seek help, because if you don't, both you and your son are at risk. If you can, enrol your son in a playgroup to give yourself more time and rest. Everytime you feel that your emotions are getting out of control, put him somewhere safe, close the door and go and make yourself a cup of tea/coffee until you have calmed down. Don't think that you could never be a child batterer, it can happen to anyone if they are stressed and pushed to the limit!*

'Hasn't Your Sister
Got a Home To Go To?'
Problems with Relations and Parents

Q My sister-in-law split up with her boyfriend and she's round at our house all the time. When I get back from work she's there, and when she's not there she's on the phone to my wife. My wife and I have no privacy any more, and she sits on my favourite chair and we all eat together. When I said to my wife 'Hasn't your sister got a home to go to?' she got very upset with me, and accused me of being hard-hearted and unsympathetic. Am I?
Greg, Wellington, N. Zealand

A *You must explain to your wife that although you are sympathetic to your sister-in-law's plight and are happy for her to visit your home, these visits must be in moderation whilst you are around. There must be plenty of time for them to meet while you are at work, and you need to have some privacy with your wife, with a chance to communicate with her when you are alone together. Your sister-in-law also needs to time to get out and meet new friends, because she will never find a new relationship sitting at home with you and your wife. If neither of them can understand your needs and refuse to compromise, suggest that maybe they might be happier living together with no interruptions from you!*

Q I recently went on holiday with my wife to visit her brother and his wife in Hong Kong. This was the first time I had met them, and within a few hours it was apparent that he and I would never have any wish to see each other again. The situation became increasingly more difficult, and one evening I had a blazing row with him and moved my wife and I out to a local hotel. I expected support from my wife, but she said she had travelled to the other side of the world to see her brother and that was what she intended to do. I couldn't believe her disloyalty to me, and I spent almost a week looking round Hong Kong on my own whilst she spent her time visiting her brother. We are now back home, but the holiday has put such a strain on our relationship that we are hardly talking to each other, and I am not sure whether I can take much more of her unreasonable behaviour. What do you advise?
Ron, Battersea

A *I advise you to apologise to your wife as soon as possible for your unreasonable behaviour. She probably doesn't see much of her brother as he lives on the other side of the world, and having made the effort and looked forward to seeing him, no-one could blame her for doing so. It was not her fault that you and your brother-in-law did not get on, and for her sake you both should have made an effort to smooth things over. If you value your marriage, then get off your 'high horse' and show some consideration for your wife now!*

Q My wife's sister is staying in our house with her two children, a boy who is nearly 5 and a 3 year old girl. In fact

they've been staying with us now for three weeks since they returned from living in South Africa, and to date there has been no mention of when they will be leaving! The biggest problem that I have with them staying with us, is the behaviour of the children. They are completely out of control, and run amock in the house always shortly after 5.30am. They break all our things, trample over the garden (I am a keen gardener) and I have come to the end of my tether. My wife sticks up for her sister and keeps telling me what a hard time she is having, and how much more sympathetic I should be towards them all. With no end to their stay with us in sight, how do I get her to control her children?
Robert, Dartmouth

A *Of course you're at the end of your tether, and you should be commended for having controlled your feelings for so long. If your wife won't discuss the problem with her sister, I suggest that you have a talk with your sister-in-law. Tell your wife when you propose to do this, so that if she wishes she can be there as well. You need to agree a date as to when they will be leaving your house, and also some ground rules on their behaviour while they are staying with you. It is your home, and however hard a time your sister-in-law is going through, she should not abuse your hospitality by letting her children run riot and wrecking it.*

Q I thought my fiancee was quite an intelligent and interesting person, but since we got married all she seems to want to do is go round to her Mum's or her sisters' (she has 4 very boring married sisters) houses for coffee. She doesn't seem to have anything to talk about any more; she gave up work and is for ever on about her sisters' kids. She is filling the house with silly frilly knick-knacks so it even *looks* like her family's homes (they all go off to craft markets and antique fairs together). I am terrified that she made some sort of special effort to 'catch' a husband, and that she is as stupid as the rest of the family. My brothers-in-law make comments about their wives which makes me suspect this, and they hate the cackling and air-headed gossip as much as me. How can I get back the girl I married, and get rid of the Ugly Sisters?
Brian, Harlow

A Why did your wife give up work? Was it a joint decision? Also the fact that she is always talking about her sisters' children and is filling the house with frilly knick-knacks may indicate that she wants children of her own soon. Is this what you want? You must both discuss your needs and wants as soon as possible, and tell her in no uncertain terms about the way you are feeling at present. You are at the beginning of your married life, and must start as you mean to go along. If you do not share the same dreams and ideals, it is better that you find out now rather than spend many years of misery together followed by a divorce. You might also like to consider moving house - as far away as possible from the in-laws!

Q My sister is too strict with her little boy. She shuts him up all the time, constantly puts him down, and is generally crushing him to such an extent that I feel she will do him lasting damage. I realise her behaviour is a symptom of her own anxiety, and that she finds it difficult bringing him up with virtually no help from his Dad (who is a merchant seaman), but I feel very concerned. Should I say anything?
Coliene, Rotterdam, Holland

A Yes you should say something to your sister if you feel so worried about your nephew. Sometimes a parent's anxiety and insecurity in their ability to bring their child up 'properly', will tip the balance and cause them to be overly strict. Your sister needs to have her confidence boosted, a listening ear for all her worries, and some practical help, so that she doesn't vent her frustrations on her child. Explain your concerns about your nephew in an unthreatening manner, and tell her that you understand why, because of her difficult circumstances, she treats her son in this way and that you want to help. Praise her for coping so well on her own, and try to find out what are her main worries. Let her know that you are always there for her as a listening ear, and that if she would like to have a bit of time off for herself, you would be willing (providing you are free) to look after your nephew whenever she needs you. Also investigate with her the possibilities of enlisting the help of other mothers, with children of the same age, to do reciprocal baby-sitting. Once she has the support of other people around her and she feels less stressed, hopefully her attitude towards your nephew will change.

Q My wife has always been very close to her Aunt who brought her up as a child, after her parents died in a car crash. Three years ago her Aunt became very frail and was unable to look after herself, and so it was a choice then of putting her into a nursing home or having her to live with us. My wife doesn't work, our children are at University, and we have a large house and I have a good income, so when my wife implored me to let her Aunt live with us, I agreed. At the time I honestly thought that her Aunt hadn't many more months to live, but three years later she's still going strong. Her presence has affected our lifestyle and our relationship. We are not free to accept invitations out on the spur of the moment, or go away for weekends because we have to make arrangements for her Aunt, and now my wife says she can't go on holiday incase anything happens to her Aunt while we are away. Also over the years I have come to feel more and more like an outsider in my own home with my wife and her Aunt being a team together, and I know our children, when they visit us, feel uncomfortable with their Aunt around all the time. What's the solution?
Kenneth, Winchester

A *Talk to your wife. She must be made to understand that you have needs and priorities as well as her Aunt. You have been more than generous in providing a home for her Aunt and disrupting your family's life, but now things must change and you need to discuss these changes with your wife. Consider employing part-time or full time help to look after her Aunt - someone that her Aunt can get used to having around and feel comfortable with. Such a person would enable you to accept invitations out, go away for weekends or go on holiday, with peace of mind that her Aunt was being well looked after. It is difficult for your wife to feel able to go away and enjoy herself when she is so full of concerns, but her Aunt has led a long and happy life and now it is time for the two of you to have happy times together. No-one knows when any of us will pass away, and so we can only do our best to ensure our own and other people's well being, and then try to enjoy every precious present moment of our own life.*

Q My sister-in-law is such a user. She's got two young kids and she's forever dumping them at a moment's notice on my in-laws (who are quite elderly and find it hard looking after them) or with me, and I've got more than enough to do with my new

baby. She borrows food and never replaces it, and borrowed our car and never told us she'd crashed it until we noticed the dent on the wing. Our baby is being Christened, and suddenly she's assumed that she can have her children done at the same time and muscle in on the party afterwards with her guests, which has already been paid for by us! She's beyond belief, we're both fed up, what do we do?
Kelly, Canterbury

A *Don't put up with any more of her inconsiderate behaviour, and advise your in-laws to do the same. Your sister-in-law will continue to carry on as before, unless you tell that you are no longer prepared to be treated in this way. You are prepared to help out occasionally with proper notice, but she must start being responsible for her own family, and make her own social arrangements in future. Do not give in to her - you are just 'making a rod for your own back', and you have more than enough to cope with already.*

'So This Is Where You Live!'
Problems with Family Friends

Q My partner is good friends with a couple that I find particularly boring. My wife looks up to them, although it is obvious to me that they feel superior to us in every way. They could barely hide their disdain when they visited our house for the first time, and you should have heard the sneer in her voice when the wife said 'So *this* is where you live!' They regale us to such an extent with details of their 'impressive' social life, that I want to scream. The main problem is that she insists on inviting them to dinner and arranging for us to go out with them. What should I do?
Rufus, Heidelberg, Germany

A *Explain your feelings to your wife, and tell her that although you are willing for her sake, to entertain or go out with this couple, it can only be occasionally. You are happy for her to see them on her own, but you would rather be elsewhere. Start filling up your wife's diary with people and social engagements that you are comfortable with, and try your best to cultivate new friends whose company both of can enjoy.*

Q My husband and I recently moved, so I joined a local gym to meet new friends. I met a girl called Joanne with whom I got on very well, and we started working out together. The problem is that the more time I spend watching her working out, I realise I am becoming sexually attracted to her. I love my husband very much and have never had any feelings for the same sex before. What shall I do?

Shaney, Montreal, Canada

A *Join another gym and forget Joanne! You do not say that Joanne has given you any indication that she is sexually interested in you, and therefore you risk making her very angry if you make advances towards her, plus causing yourself a lot of embarrassment. Don't risk your marriage for a brief flirtation which might not even be reciprocated!*

Q A couple we have been friendly with for over ten years are going through a very bitter divorce. Each of them look upon us as their special friends and would get upset if they knew we were seeing the other. We like them both and want to stay friends with both of them, but how can we, without making the other feel that we are being disloyal to them?

Marjorie, Bridgport

A *You have to be honest with both of them, and tell them that whatever differences they may have it is a private matter for them, and as such is none of your concern. You consider both of them to be your special friends and would like to keep it that way; you do not wish to be asked to take sides. If you cannot see them together any more, you hope they will realise that you are loyal to both of them and therefore would like to still see each of them on their own.*

Q When my girlfriend's marriage broke up I befriended her, and she, my husband and I became very close. We took her everywhere, and all three of us were so close that we even used to lie on our bed watching the TV with my husband between the two us, with his arm around each of us. I trusted my husband completely, and always used to boast to my girlfriend that he was 'steady as a rock' and a 'cut above' other men. I work as a singer, and a few weeks ago I went up North to do a week's cabaret in a hotel. It was a good engagement and I wanted to do it, and although I didn't want to leave home for a week I asked my friend to look after my husband whilst I was away. I certainly didn't expect her to look after him in the way she did! When I got back she took great delight in telling me that my husband was no different from other men, and gave me an intimate account of what they had got up to. My whole world has crumpled and I feel totally betrayed by both of them. What shall I do?

Glenys, Egham

A Discard your girlfriend for a start, and learn a lesson from this painful episode never to be so naive as to hand your husband over 'on a plate' to any woman, especially whilst you are away. They have both betrayed your trust, and you will find it difficult to build up trust in your husband again; you need to have serious discussions with your husband about his conduct if you are to have any future together. If he can convince you that this was an isolated incident which he really regrets, and it will never happen again, then give him another chance - one slip is not worth a marriage. If he ever betrays you a second time, don't let him see you for dust!

Q I am writing to you for advice about my friend. She is very beautiful, in her mid forties, and is married to a retired man 20 years her senior. She is very sociable and wants to go out all the time, but he just wants to watch the TV or play golf with his chums. He only likes to watch sport on TV, and as she does not like watching sport she spends a lot of time watching her TV in the kitchen, usually while she is cooking endless meals for him. They seem to have no common interests, they never go out together, but he wants sex at every available opportunity with her. However although she always complies with this, she doesn't fancy him! She made the best of her life up until last summer when she came away on holiday with me. I am divorced and live with my son, but her

husband always welcomed the friendship between us, and was happy to let her see me whenever she liked. On holiday she had an affair, and now she is even more dissatisfied with her marriage. She has always written down everything that happens to her in her diary, and last week her husband read it and found out about the affair. I have told her not to write a diary any more, but she knows that her husband is reading through her old diaries as well. He had an affair two years ago which he excuses on the grounds that it was just pure lust, unlike hers which was not. Although I was also good friends with her husband, he now disapproves of me and says that I am a bad influence on her. She can now only ring me when he goes out, and we meet in secret once a week. He is completely paranoid and the lovemaking has increased. She is very unhappy and would like to leave him, but she doesn't want to hurt him; also they are not very well off. I am very worried about my friend; how can I help?
Amanda, Cheltenham

A *Your friend has already hurt her husband; people who leave their diaries lying around, usually mean them to be read. I think your friend probably wants her husband to leave her, so that she can appear to be the injured party. If your friend finds it impossible to discuss things with her husband, she might as well write down exactly how she feels now and leave these notes with her old diaries. I suspect she is also terrified of being single and financially independent, and she may feel that a bad marriage is preferable to being on her own. It would be best for your friend to persuade her husband that they are facing major difficulties in their marriage, and that they should go together to a Marriage Guidance Counsellor to see if they can salvage their relationship. If he refuses to go with her, she should go as soon as possible to see a counsellor on her own to sort out her own feelings, and to give her the courage to follow the right course of action. You can find the telephone number of Relate in your local phone directory, and maybe you could support your friend by accompanying her to the first consultation. Her husband obviously feels that you are no friend of his having 'condoned' his wife's affair on holiday, and is very insecure and scared of losing his wife and his finances - he needs help as well, and maybe you could somehow indicate to him that you would like to help them both.*

Q I feel that it is really important to keep in touch with my old friends even though my partner doesn't get on with them. He has fallen out with most of them and sees it as a betrayal of our relationship if I see them on my own or even contact them. I am feeling very depressed about the situation, what shall I do?
Pat, Lowestoft

A Beware of your partner, he sounds like a 'control freak'! If he cared enough for you, he would try his best to be pleasant and polite to your friends so as to keep you happy. If he really can't stand being with them, allocate yourself one evening a week to see them on your own. It is outrageous of him to tell you who you can or cannot contact or see, and if he won't respect your wishes, you would be better off looking for someone less selfish who really cares for you.

Q We are very friendly with a couple who are going through a stormy patch in their marriage. I am the wife's confidante and my husband is her husband's confidante. We are finding that their problems are beginning to cause problems for us because we both are sworn to secrecy by each warring side, which means that we have to watch what we say to each other in case we disclose any information which one side wanted to keep from the other. I feel that their problems are causing a barrier between us, and I don't like it. I don't like not being able to confide in my husband, but I don't want to let my friend down. What's the solution?
Moira, Cumbria

A I think that you both have to tell your friends (in the nicest possible way) that although you are prepared to listen to their problems, you can no longer agree to keep their confidences from your 'other half'. Explain that their confidences are causing a barrier between you and your husband, and you are sure that they would not want your marriage to go through a similar stormy patch to theirs because of them.

SEX

'The Spirit's Willing But The Body Can't Cope!' Problems Men have with their sex-life at any age

Q I had a prostate gland operation last year and can no longer get an erection. I really miss making love to my wife and I know she resents the fact that her sex life has now ceased. She repudiates all my compliments and laughs at me when I say I love her, and now she never says she loves me. Even though the spirit's willing but the body can't cope, I still need her affection. How can I win it back?
Eric, Hailsham

A You could ask your Doctor about alternative ways of getting an erection through artificial aids, and of course there are many ways in which you can pleasure your wife without penetration - buy a few books on the subject. However I would advise you to ask your GP to arrange for you both to have psycho-sexual counselling, to enable you to sort out your relationship problems as well as your sex life.

Q My girlfriend and I, both 18, have been seeing each other for just over a year. She's the first and only girl I have ever had a sexual relationship with, and I thought everything was great. We both started at different Universities two months ago, and we met up for the first time last night. My girlfriend admitted to having had a one night stand a few weeks ago, and told me that she no longer wanted sex with me as she had not known how 'small' I was in comparison to other men, and felt that I could no longer satisfy her. I am devastated, hurt and humiliated, and I don't think I can ever face trying to have another sexual relationship again as I am apparently so inadequate. Is there an operation I could have to enlarge what little I have? Please advise.
Nigel, Hampstead

A *There is an operation that you could have to make you bigger, but I certainly wouldn't advise you to go through with it. What's too small for this girlfriend may be just right for the next; we all have to find the right fit for us, and if you were too big you would have had the same problem - not every key opens every lock! Bear in mind that the Rolls Royce car does very well in popularity, but the Mini was an immediate success and everyone wanted it! You are perfectly normal and this is your girlfriend's problem, not yours. Also remember that it is not necessarily what you have which counts, but what you do with it. You had a good sex life with your girlfriend for a year, and I'm sure you will have an even better one with the next.*

Q My wife and I hardly ever have sex any more. She works hard at her job as well as looking after our two children, and I know she gets really tired. Whenever I try to initiate sex she just turns over and says she's exhausted; on the few times she has wanted sex, I haven't been ready for her. I'm feeling very tense about the whole situation, but I do not want to have extra-marital sex to make up for it. I was always taught at school that masturbation is a sin, what shall I do?
Patrick, Limerick

A *Masturbation is not a sin, and it would probably make you feel less tense at present if you were to do it. More importantly though, I think that you should organise a weekend away with your wife, something exciting for the children so that they don't feel rejected, and relax and enjoy yourselves. Try to give your wife some help round the house or employ some domestic help for her so that she gets less tired. Also set aside one night a week when you can take her out, and generally give her more attention. Don't forget that people are usually less tired in the morning, so why don't you both wake up earlier and initiate sex then?*

Q My girlfriend only gets an orgasm when we make love in public places. She wants me to take more and more risks but I'm terrified of getting arrested for indecency. Sadly, making love at home no longer excites her. How can I get some normality back into our sex-life?
Spencer, Santiago, U.S.A.

A Your girlfriend seems to only get turned on by taking risks and can probably never change. So you have two choices: either find a different risk or find another girlfriend. Above all you must make sure you that you never do anything that you don't want to do.

Q My wife insists that we both have to shower before making love, and as soon as we've made love she leaps out of bed to shower again. She says that personal hygiene is very important, but I would rather she stayed with me in bed and had a cuddle. I feel rejected by her washing off the results of our love-making with such urgency. How can I change this fetish of hers?
Helmut, Koln, Germany

A Does she realise how you feel, have you ever told her? If this has been a lifetime habit she's unlikely to change it completely, however ask her to compromise by putting off having the second shower for 15 minutes so that your feelings are less hurt. Also initiate sex sometimes where there is no shower available within walking distance! It could be that she a deep-rooted feeling that sex is a dirty act (this often happens if someone has been sexually abused as a child), and if you were to try making love in the shower, it might help get round her problem of feeling dirty.

Q I get so overexcited whenever I am near my girlfriend that sex only lasts a few seconds before I ejaculate. My girlfriend is very understanding, but I think she's getting fed up with the situation. Help!
Michael, Reading

A *Premature ejaculation affects a great number of men at some point in their lives. I am sure that this is only a temporary problem, and that once you stop worrying about the situation and become more familiar with your girlfriend, everything will be alright. In the meantime give your girlfriend pleasure manually and orally as well. Maybe it's worth discussing this issue with your GP, and then if he feels that you would benefit from specific advice he can refer you appropriately. Also consider looking in the backs of magazines where there are catalogues for sex accessories which can often assist this situation.*

Q I love my girlfriend very much and I know she loves me in return. We have been going out for six months but have never managed to have sex with each other yet, and she tells me that she has never been able to have sex with anyone. Whenever I try to penetrate her, her vaginal muscles just go into spasm and it is totally impossible. She is too embarrassed to talk to anyone about this, and I am at my wits end to know what to do. Any suggestions?
Jim, Beckenham

A *This is not an uncommon problem in women and it has a medical name - Vaginismus. It is usually due to a fear of being hurt, or it might even be a form of sexual guilt. Tell your girlfriend that she can be helped, but only if she is prepared to seek it. Suggest that she makes an appointment with her local GP, and that as you are involved as well you would like to be there with her. Her GP will then be able to refer her for the appropriate help which she needs. Good Luck, this should not be an insurmountable problem.*

Q My girlfriend doesn't like wearing underwear of any description, and although this excites me in private, I get embarrassed when, for example, we are dancing in a Disco and everyone else gets a glimpse as well. When she sees how embarrassed I am she becomes more outrageous than ever, and then when we get

home she keeps me at arms' length and denies me any sex. I feel hurt and confused and would value your advice.
Jean-Claude, Paris

A Get rid of her! She's behaving outrageously towards you and being extremely cruel. Find yourself a new sexy girlfriend who also has a heart!

'On Top of the Stove? You Can't Be Serious - Can You?'
Problems Women have with their sex-life at any age.

Q My boyfriend keeps trying to make love to me in different parts of the house and I'm terrified that someone might see us. The other day I was about to start cooking dinner, when he purposefully approached me and I said 'Not on top of the stove? You can't be serious - can you?' He was, and I'm sure that the whole neighbourhood saw us through the kitchen window. I feel so embarrassed now whenever I see my neighbours. I don't want to reject him, but I'm finding the situation impossible to deal with. Please advise.
Sonia, Cheam

A *Install blinds on the windows that can be quickly pulled down at a moment's notice, and enjoy yourself. Don't reject him sexually, because he might eventually get fed up and reject you as a person. Also don't be embarrassed with the neighbours, they are probably extremely envious of your exciting sex-life!*

Q My husband's chums have been bragging to him about their sex-lives, and now he's convinced that he's missed out on life by not having been to bed with two women at the same time. He has become obsessed by this idea, and tells me that his secretary has expressed an interest in other women. He's trying to persuade me to go to bed with her so that he can have us both! I don't fancy his secretary or indeed any other female. Am I abnormal or is he?
Jean, Dartington

A *You are not abnormal and neither necessarily is he. Most men fantasise about something different in their sex-life, and the two women syndrome is one of the most popular fantasies. It is up to you what you do about it, because giving in to his wishes will either get it out of his system, or convince him that this is the only way to have sex. You should never be persuaded to do anything that you don't wish to do. It can only make you unhappy, and resentful of the other person.*

Q As our sex-life started to wane, my husband and I began watching sex films. Now it seems he can't get an erection without visual stimulation from a magazine or video. I used to find such films and magazines equally exciting but now they seem boring, and watching others perform no longer turns me on. Does this mean we are now incompatible?
Betty, Lancaster

A *You are only incompatible in your viewing habits, but so are many couples; not everyone likes 'Coronation Street'. This certainly doesn't mean that you are sexually incompatible. If you want to read a book while he watches a pornographic film, what does it matter so long as the sexual results are good for both of you?*

Q Whenever we make love, my boyfriend's condom slips off. All the condoms he's tried seem to be the same size; is it possible to get a different size?
Lyn, Harrogate

A *Yes it is. If your local stores don't stock them, phone mail order companies such as Condomania (tele: 01635 874393) or the Condom Store (tele: 01273 746273) who will be able to help you.*

Q My husband demands sex from me two or three times a night and I'm exhausted! I desperately need some sleep, and I long to wake up without him bouncing around all over me. Is there anything I can do to make me less sexually attractive to him?
Deirdre, Bolton

A You could put a mud pack on your face just before you go to bed; spray yourself with insect repellent and eat lots of garlic and onions! Seriously though, making yourself less sexually attractive to your husband is not the answer. You need to tell him how you feel and discuss the problem. Everyone's sex drive is different and we all need varying amounts of sleep. Suggest that your husband joins a gym or plays more sport to tire himself out, and whenever he is sexually desperate during the night he could masturbate. Don't discourage him too much - you don't want him to supplement his needs elsewhere!

Q A few weeks ago my boyfriend and I had sex for the first time and I really enjoyed it. However since then he has been reluctant to let me see his body. He insists on getting undressed in the bathroom and turning out the light in the bedroom before he comes to bed in his pyjamas. How can I persuade him that he has nothing to be ashamed of?
Sian, Swansea

A You could try putting a dimmer switch on the bedroom light to make the light less harsh, or light candles in the bedroom while he is in the bathroom to make the scene more romantic Then discuss the problem with him and tell him how much he turns you on. Maybe he's shy and lacking in confidence, so tell him that whatever he may think are his shortcomings they are immaterial to you, and you just want him. Have you ever wondered how many times he'd had sex before the first time with you?

Q I have been married to my husband for 15 years and care for him a great deal. Recently we were at a dinner party at some new neighbours' house when they suggested partner swapping. We were all very drunk and eventually I reluctantly agreed with a lot of coaxing from my husband. The problem is that the sex was so

good with my neighbour that I want to do it again! My husband
says it was all a ghastly mistake and that we should never do it again.
What should I do?
Donna, Birmingham

*A Your husband is right this time. It was a mistake for you
both to have sex with your neighbours, and if you value your
marriage and wish it to continue, I suggest you do not participate again.
I do feel concerned that your husband originally encouraged you to have
sex with another man, presumably because he wanted to have sex with
this man's wife. Now that the adventure has backfired and he is upset
that you prefer sex with your neighbour (whilst I suspect his sexual
encounter the wife was less favourable), do you feel you can trust him
again, and will you ever let yourself be persuaded again into doing
something that you don't want to do? You both need to have serious
talks about your future, and I think it would be a good idea to go away
for a weekend or holiday with him as soon as possible to try to repair the
damage that has been done to your marriage and trust in one another.
You say you care for him a great deal, and I imagine you used to enjoy
your sex life with him, therefore hopefully you can recapture your sexual
interest in him if you have the determination to do so. If however you
decide to continue to have sex again with your neighbour, you may well
find that he is just using you because he no longer finds his wife sexually
attractive, and you may lose your self respect as well as your husband.*

Q Over the years my husband and I have tried many
different ways to perk up our sex-life, and one of them was
with him wearing my clothes. Now he doesn't seem to want to
have sex in any other way, and the other day I saw him putting on
his city trousers over my stockings and suspenders. I'm beginning
to worry about him, what shall I do?
Felicity, Wolverhampton

*A Don't worry. If he finds wearing your clothes exciting and
stimulating, so that your sex-life is improved when he gets back
home by him being turned on all day, then it's your gain. However if he
comes home tired, not wanting as much sex as usual, there may be cause
for concern. If this is the case, then like all problems it is best met head
on. Ask him why, if dressing up in your clothes excites him so much,*

there hasn't been a massive increase in sex at home. Tell him that you don't mind him putting on your stockings and suspenders to excite him for you, but it is beyond the pale for him to wear them to get him excited for someone else.

SINGLE AGAIN

'How Do I Boil This Egg?'
Problems Experienced by Men

Q My wife has left me and our two children for another man. Apart from the obvious grief we are all suffering, I feel completely lost and helpless. My wife was the most capable woman I have ever known, and looking back on it I suppose I just took her for granted. She did everything and even bought my clothes. I don't know how to work the washing machine, where to shop - I don't even know how to boil an egg! My children look to me to fill her role and I just can't cope. Please help.
Bill, Horley

A This has obviously been an extremely traumatic blow to you, but you do need to get someone in as soon as possible to show you how to use the household gadgets. If you can afford it, get some domestic help in the house, and a babysitter to enable you to go to cookery classes. Enlist your children's help in the home as much as possible, and try making it a fun game 'playing house' with you. In future you must take equal responsibility for household chores, so that in the next relationship you are not totally dependent on the other person.

Q When I first split up with my wife, my friends' wives rallied round and did their best to cheer me up and support me. Now that I have cheered up and am beginning to enjoy single life they seem to resent it. They see my happiness as a threat to them because they fear their husbands may reflect on the state of their own marriage. How can I help them overcome this?
Johann, Salzburg, Austria

A Make a point of telling them, in front of their husbands, how grateful you are for their support when you felt at your lowest ebb, and that it is all due to them that you are now feeling happier and have come to terms with being single. However, you envy their marriages and happiness together, and would swap your single state for their married bliss any day. Tell them that you now realise how wrong you were (when you were married yourself) to imagine that the grass was greener on the other side. They'll love it, and you'll be more popular than ever!

Q I was recently divorced after 10 years in a loveless marriage. A few weeks after the divorce I went out for a drink with Gemma who works near me, and we ended up in bed together. The evening was so special that we started spending every moment with each other, wrote love letters when we were apart, and planned to buy a house together as soon as possible. In the New Year I had two ski holidays booked which I could not get out of. We missed each other so much and made numerous phone calls, but during the second holiday, after one of these calls, she went to bed with a colleague from work. I knew something was wrong when I returned from holiday, but she didn't tell me for a week. When I found out I wanted to carry on seeing her because I love her so much, but she feels so guilty she won't see me anymore and doesn't even return my calls. Why am I being punished for her indiscretions?
Neville, Bournemouth

A *Poor you, you came straight out of the frying pan into the fire! You needed to find love and romance at the end of your divorce, and maybe if Gemma had come along at some other time, things might not have moved so quickly. Maybe she was overwhelmed and frightened off by the intensity of the situation, and was not ready for such a commitment in so short a time. Maybe her way of escape was to go to bed with another whilst you were away, hoping that your relationship would end once she told you about it - and I really think she has ended this relationship. Remember the good times you had together, and realise that these feelings can be recreated with someone else in the future, when hopefully you will feel calmer and not rush into things. Your relationship with Gemma has served its purpose and got you over the divorce. Think of this relationship as being an excellent stepping stone to a happier and more successful one next time.*

Q I have been divorced for 18 months, but since I have been single I know I have broken up three of my friends' marriages and I feel very concerned. Each time I have met a new girlfriend and been 'head over heels' in love with her, married friends have asked us to come and stay with them for a short break. Within months of our visit their marriage has broken up. I feel that my visits must be the 'kiss of death' to any marriage, and I am afraid to accept any more invitations. What are your views?
Charles, Keswick

A *Be selective about which friends you go to stay with in future. Make sure that they are couples which you know have established happy marriages. Staying with couples who may be feeling a little restless with each other, and letting them see, through your happy relationship, what is lacking from their own, is bound to 'upset the apple cart'.*

Q After 20 years of marriage I am now on my own. I am inundated with invitations to dinner parties from wives anxious to matchmake their single girlfriends - I seem to be a commodity that has to be paired off with any available female. I'm just not ready yet, and I feel awkward with the situation; I am still feeling bruised from my marriage break-up. Why can't my friends understand that I just want *their* company?
Les, Doncaster

A *I am sure your friends are only trying their best to help you, and they think that finding you someone else who will make you happy, as soon as possible, is the best way to do this. Therefore you must explain to them that you are not ready for this kind of help yet, and that what you really need is just their company and support. If they can give you a little time to get over the marriage break-up in your own way, then you will be grateful for new introductions at a later date.*

Q I'm 45 years old with a good job, and I'm not bad looking I'm told! However I'm on my fourth divorce now, and I'm getting worried I will never find the right person to settle down with. My relationships always start off great, but in the end I get dissatisfied, irritable, nit-picking and angry. Please advise.
Glen, Arkansas, U.S.A.

A *Although you may not realise it, you probably put on an act that is not the 'real you' when you first meet someone, and the vibes you give out attract a certain type. Eventually when you relax, drop the pretence and become your real self, you become dissatisfied, irritated, nit-picking and angry, because you're not with the right kind of person for the 'real you'. You need to take time out on your own to find out who the 'real you' is, what makes you feel comfortable and what you like to do. When you really know who you are and what you want from life, set out on your quest again, but as soon as you recognise you are behaving out of character don't make the same old mistakes again, and change direction as soon as possible.*

Q I lost my wife in a car accident 12 years ago. I brought up my children alone, and until recently when the youngest moved out, I hadn't really thought about being single. I started to feel lonely so I began going out and meeting women. It was very hard at first, but I have now met a wonderful woman who is not at all like my late wife. Part of me wants to settle down with her (she is keen to get married), but even after all this time part of me still feels I would be betraying my wife. It even affects our lovemaking as I feel like I'm being unfaithful. I feel I have done everything I could for the children, and logically I should now make a new life for myself. So why can't I let go of the past?
Ricardo, Alicante, Spain

A *If it had been you who had died in the accident and not your wife, would you have wanted her to spend the rest of her life feeling guilty and not having the chance to find happiness with someone else? Loving your wife as you did, I'm sure you would have just wanted her to be happy, and if she had found someone to give her that happiness she would have had your blessing. Therefore there is no reason why your loving wife would have felt any differently towards you, and so please consider that you have her blessing to get on with enjoying the present and future together with your new 'wonderful woman'. You are a lucky man to have been given such a second chance for happiness, so grab hold of it while you can.*

Q I have been going out on my own with my male friends for years, but now I have got divorced their wives and girlfriends see me as a threat. They seem to think that as I now single I must be on the hunt for women, and therefore if their husbands are with me I will influence them to do the same. Am I now to be denied even the company of my friends?
Ravi, Bayswater

A *Try to make sure that whatever activities and outings you get up to with your 'attached' male friends, are ones that the wives* *and girlfriends know are purely male oriented, where there are no available single females present! Also let them feel that they have an open invitation to come and join you all at any time. Try to make your life sound fairly mundane when you talk to them, and suggest that they help you find a new woman who will make you as happy as know your mates are with them!*

Q I've just got divorced after 15 years of marriage and I feel completely lost. I've always been a socially confident person, never at a loss for words, but now I find I don't know how to behave in female company any more. If I like a woman I don't know how to ask her out; should I ask for her telephone number or give her my card? I don't want to be rejected but I don't want to miss out. If I do go out on a date how do I behave? Should I buy her flowers? Do we kiss? Do we make love on the first night? I need your advice.
Peter, Godalming

A *There are no set rules, just be yourself. Some women will feel more secure, if there are no mutual contacts, by taking your card instead of giving their phone number. In this case try to arrange a firm date with her before you say good-bye. Otherwise offer your personal card for her to write down her name and telephone number on it, with a view to you calling her (of course she has the option of writing down a false number if she does not wish you to have the real one). Flowers are always a good idea, but after that you are on your own; you will either find that you have interests in common which make the evening go with a swing, or you don't. If you want to kiss her and think that your feelings are reciprocated, then do it. It is never a good idea to make a point of trying to go to bed with someone on the first date. Sometimes it happens but it is not a good recipe for a long term relationship, because at some later date you may reflect on how 'easy' your partner was when you first met her, and then start to distrust her in the company of others. Just be patient with yourself, and don't worry if you make a few mistakes - you're only human. The more practice you have, the quicker your confidence will return.*

'Daddy's Gone Away'
Problems Experienced by Women

Q My husband of 12 years left me 6 weeks ago - he's moved in with another woman. I have now got over the initial shock, but the problem is that I haven't yet told the children the true situation. At first (before I knew he was with someone else) I believed that Derek would come back, so I saw no sense in upsetting the children (ages 10 and 8) and I sent them to stay with Mum and Dad for a while. When the kids came back, my in-laws tried to persuade Derek to come home and then the truth came to light. I couldn't cope with the news, and I decided to spend a few days at my Mum's to try to hang on to my sanity. Luckily my in-laws sided with me, and they came to look after the children at our house whilst we pretended to the kids that Derek and I had gone on holiday. During all this time Derek has not seen the children but has spoken to them on the phone. He has told the children nothing as well, because he says that as they are living with me it's up to me to tell them. I knew I could only make excuses for a few days when I got back from my Mum's. I tried to explain to the children but I never got past 'Daddy's gone away for a while'; I didn't want to break down in front of them so I said nothing more and just fobbed off their questions. This is so unfair - why should I be the one feeling guilty for hurting them? How can I tell them the truth after all these excuses? The longer this goes on, the harder it gets. Whatever can I do?
June, Epsom

A *If Derek is not coming home your children will have to know soon, and they also need to see him. The fact that they have not seen him for a while, and must have got used to life without him, will help. They will obviously be hurt whenever they are told, and it is important not to apportion blame to anyone - just try to make things as painless as possible for them. Tell them that Daddy has decided, for reasons of his own, that he would prefer to live with his new friend rather than with you, and that it is no reflection on you or them, it is his choice at this time. Life will be different from the way it was before, and it may be even better for them. Their Daddy still loves them and wants to see them soon, but in future they will spend time with him and his new friend in their home and have lots of fun , and they will live at home with you and have lots of fun - they will have two happy homes, with parents in each that really love them. There are bound to be tears, and it might be a good idea to have their grandparents around to help you comfort them, and to distract them. Always make sure that you and Derek put up a happy front in their presence, back each other up at all times, and that neither of you attempts to make the children take sides against the other. Yes all this is unfair on you, but so is life - take heart, you'll win through.*

Q I am 45 years old and after thirteen years of marriage I am going through a divorce - my husband left me for a younger woman. I feel such a failure, I can't face my friends and I've lost all my self confidence. I am scared I will never meet anyone else again to share my life with, and I am getting more and more depressed. What is the answer?
Sheila, Keston

A It is natural for you to feel so wretched because you have suffered a bereavement - the loss of your marriage, and you must give yourself a period of mourning. Divorce is not unique to you alone, and I am sure your friends are not seeing you as a failure and are not blaming you. Let them know how you are feeling and give them a chance to show their support for you. There is always a tendency to feel desperate if you have been rejected, but please resist the urge to search for or dive into a new relationship. There is plenty of time and plenty of men out there! Do some work on yourself - consider changing your image, and if you can spare the time take up a sport or start a new hobby, and read. When you eventually feel at peace with yourself and are happy with your own company, then consider letting someone else enter into your life - that is when you'll find others start being attracted to you. When you have reached this stage, join a reputable singles dining and social events club where you will probably meet more eligible prospective partners than you can possibly cope with!

Q Please help me I'm so confused, and constantly in such a nervous state I don't know what to do. I have two children, and after the birth of my second child my breasts shrank to half their normal size and sagged. This upset my husband so much he persuaded me to have implants, and although the operation was successful and we both loved the new look me, it caused

insurmountable problems. I didn't like him touching my breasts; I was terrified of any pressure on them, and I know I made my husband feel rejected so that in the end he resented the fact that they were not natural. We eventually divorced, and now I am terrified of intimacy with another man in case I experience the same feelings, which might make the new man in my life feel the same way as my ex-husband. What's the solution?
Val, Kew

A You now have a very beautiful body which you are proud of at the same time as being frightened of, and you need professional help to overcome this problem. Go back to your surgeon, explain your feelings and fears and seek his advice. He will reassure you about the sturdiness of the implants and maybe refer you for some counselling advice. You were persuaded to have the operation by your ex-husband, and if you eventually decide that you can't cope with the implants, the operation can be reversed. I would then suggest that you only settle for a man who does not want to change your body shape, and likes and accepts you as you really are.

Q My husband treated me very badly during our marriage and our friends used to sympathise with me, and then he left me with all his debts. I would have thought that out of loyalty to me they would have nothing to do with him now that we are divorced, but I've heard that at least two couples have invited him round to dinner with them, and I can't believe their disloyalty to me. How can I ever have anything to do with them again?
Suki, Hong Kong

A They were friends with both of you while you were married, so why should they not be friends with you both now that you are divorced? You shouldn't expect your friends to take sides. If you decide that you still want them to be friends with you, try not to mention your problems when you see them. Your friends can sympathise with you up to a point, but then they probably have enough problems of their own to think about, and your husband's debts are best sorted out by you, your ex-husband and lawyers.

Q I am recently divorced, and have been dating a divorced man who I have fallen in love with. The trouble is that I hate children and never intended to have any, but he has made it very clear that he wants a big family as soon as possible. Also the reason he split up with his ex-wife was because she couldn't have children. I love him and would do anything within reason to keep him. What do you advise?
Stephanie, Bradford

A *Any relationship is a non-starter if you don't share the same dreams and ultimate goals. I would advise you to have professional counselling as to why you hate children, and whether or not you would think differently if the children were your own. Many parents who dote on their own children, have little time for other people's! If after counselling you still dislike the thought of children, and cannot contemplate having any of your own, you must tell your boyfriend. Better to part now, rather than deceive him and suffer another divorce later.*

Q My husband died unexpectedly three months ago from a heart attack and I just can't come to terms with his death, and also with being on my own again after so many happy years of marriage. My friends are wonderful to me and very supportive, and although they ask me round to visit them and try to introduce me to 'new men', I would rather stay in by myself and think about my husband. How can I cope with this awful emptiness I feel inside me?
Elspeth, Bletchley

A *Three months is very early days, and it is very natural for you to miss him - you really do need to give yourself enough time to grieve. It would be a good idea to talk to someone experienced to help you, and CRUSE, the organisation for the bereaved, would be happy to do that. Phone 0181 940 4818 for details of your local CRUSE group, or their helpline on 0181 332 7227 (weekdays 9.30am to 5pm). When you feel ready, look for details in your local library of day or evening classes to join to help fill the gap. You will also find that exercise is very beneficial. Time is a great healer; just be patient with yourself and you will eventually cope and be able to face life without your husband.*

Q Although our sex life has been non existent for many years because I went off it, I love my husband very much and I thought he loved me. Five weeks ago after we had finished having dinner one night, he told me that he didn't want to be my husband any more, just my best friend. I was devastated and pleaded with him to tell me that he loved me, and he said he didn't know if he did. I asked him if there was someone else in his life and he said 'no'. He moved out the next day, and since then I have gone to pieces although he phones me every day. I have just found out that there is another woman in his life, and I have begged my husband to allow me to become his mistress. I have pretended that I can accept the fact that he is with her, and that I just want to be with him whenever he needs me. I will do anything so as not to lose him. I am going out of my mind with despair. The children keep phoning him up and telling him not to make me cry, but it does no good. Please help.
Nina, Brussels, Belgium

A *I can imagine how awful you must feel, but please don't lose your dignity by throwing yourself at your husband - it won't win him back and he may lose his respect for you. However desperate you may feel, try your best to hide your unhappiness from your children. Their phone calls to your husband will not help your cause with him, and will probably anger him. Also your problems are between the two of you, and it is unfair and upsetting for the children to involve them. If you had been entirely happy with your husband during your marriage, I don't think that you would have 'gone off' your sex life with him five years ago. I think what you are experiencing now is terror at the thought of being single again, and not having the support and social acceptance of a husband by your side. I know that life must look very frightening and bleak to you at present, with the inevitable prospect of divorce and all that entails looming ahead, but from one who has been through it all, I can assure you that the fear is worse than the reality. Talk to your friends for support, get some counselling, and distance yourself from your husband. Although he obviously still cares for you and phones you every day, he has chosen for whatever reason, to be with someone else, and you must be brave and step forward to make a new life for yourself and for your children. One day you may thank your husband for being brave enough to end your marriage, and for giving you the chance to meet someone different who will make you even happier than he did. Life is offering you new exciting opportunities, so grab hold of them as soon as you can.*

Q I have been divorced for 18 months and have an 8 year old son called Mark. My husband (Chris) left me to live with his girlfriend, and he was always so wrapped up in her that he let Mark down all the time. For example he would arrange to take him out for the day, and Mark would wait by the front door for hours on end for his daddy to arrive, which of course he never did. He would make arrangements to have Mark for the weekend, and at the last minute phone up and cancel. Although Mark used to cry his eyes out, he always accepted whatever excuses his father chose to give him. My heart used to bleed for him and I wanted to tell him what a bastard his father was, but I always kept quiet. A few months ago Chris' relationship with his girlfriend broke up, and he made arrangements to take Mark away for a holiday of a lifetime to Disney World for three weeks. I was thrilled for Mark's sake because he was so excited to go away at last with his father, and although I knew I would miss him desperately I cheerfully waved him on his way. Mark arrived back three days ago, and life has been a nightmare ever since. He doesn't want to know me! He says he wants to live with his daddy because his daddy loves him and I don't! He says his daddy spent more money on him in three weeks than I have in a year, and therefore he must love him more than I do. My heart is breaking and I don't know what to do. Please help!
Janice, Hereford

A *Explain to Mark that money is not love, and that you would love to be able to give him such treats but you can't afford it. All you can afford to give him is your time and love, and he has always been given lots of that. It is always very easy for the parent not living at home, to appear to be the 'goody'. Explain the situation to Chris and try to enlist his help. Just be patient, these are early days and I am sure that once Mark has got back into his old routines things will be back to normal between you. When he is older he will realise and appreciate just who gave the most to him during his childhood!*

Q My husband and I have split up and we are getting divorced. I know we are doing the right thing because we have been unhappy with each other for so long, and our marriage was destroying us both. However I never realised how alone I would feel as a single woman. My female married friends view me as a

predator - they are suspicious of me and think I am going to try to steal their husbands. As for the husbands - some of them have already propositioned me, seeing me as easy game, desperate for sex at any cost! Nothing is further from my mind; I just need my friends. I feel wretched, what can I do?
Hayley, Knutsford

A I don't think you need the kind of friendship that your 'friends' are offering. You need to start again and make a new life for yourself, which includes making new friends. Go to places where you know there are single people; join a gym or sports club, go to evening classes, or join a reputable singles dining and social events club. The world is full of single people who would like to befriend you; just enjoy the adventure of finding them.

'Was It All My Fault?'
Problems experienced by Children

Q Mummy and Daddy have told me they are going to get divorced and Daddy has left home. They used to quarrel a lot, and I'm sure most of the time it was about me. I wasn't always good, and Daddy used to shout at Mummy and say she was too soft with me and let me get away with murder. Mummy would cry but she always stood up for me, and after a while things would get better. If only I had known how bad things were and that my behaviour would split them up, I would have tried much harder to be better. Now it's too late and Daddy's gone, and I hate myself for what I've done to them. Was it all my fault?
Harry, Wensleydale

A No, it was not your fault at all. For whatever personal reasons they may have, your Mummy and Daddy have decided that it would be better and happier for all of you if they no longer live together. They both still love you very much and will stay friends with each other, but from now on you will spend time with each of them separately. Whenever there is a loss of any kind we always blame ourselves, but there is no blame - things just happen. Eventually you will come to realise that they made the right decision, and it is better to be happy with each parent on their own, than live in an unhappy home with both of them.

Q My parents just got divorced and they feel very bitter about each other. I feel I'm being asked to choose between them, and if I say too much about one I hurt the other. I want to talk about everything with both of them, but I feel disloyal by letting Dad know what Mum's doing, and unfair to Mum by saying what a good time I've just had with Dad. Please help.
Kieran, Cheshunt

A *This is entirely your parents' problem, not yours. You must feel free to talk about any part of your life to either parent, without being afraid of offending them. Be tactful and never deliberately hurt either of them, and just try to be yourself. When you see your Dad tell him how much you've missed him, and when you come home to Mum after a visit to Dad, give her an extra hug and let her know how much you love her. Give them time to get over the divorce, and hopefully life between them will become more normal.*

Q I am 11½ years old and my parents are getting divorced and there's a custody hearing. I've been told that I've got to say who I want to be with, but I love them both. I don't know who to choose, so I'm thinking of running away so I don't hurt either of them. What do you think?
James, Cheshire

A *What you are talking about is nowadays called a residence order, and you do not have to make any choice. Before there is any formal hearing or statements there is something called a conciliatory hearing where a Judge and a Welfare Officer sits down informally with you and your parents, just to try to find out what's best for you. Nobody fights, and at your age you are old enough for someone to listen to what you think as well as to what your parents think. The Judge or Welfare Officer will also have a friendly chat with you on your own, and it is very important to remember that what you say is private between you and them, and not even your parents will know what you said unless you want them to. Deciding what's best for you is a very complicated matter (just as at home you don't always know what's best for you), but what all of you want will be taken into consideration, and hopefully at this meeting it can all be agreed and sorted out. It is only in cases where things cannot be sorted out that everything becomes more formal, and hearings take place and decisions are reached not by agreement. Running away can only make matters worse, and might even convince the courts that you do not want to live with either parent!*

Q I took a year out after I finished my degree course at University, to travel and work abroad. I have just arrived back home and am appalled at the situation here. My father was under so much pressure at work that he had a nervous breakdown, my mother took to the bottle because she couldn't cope with him, and my sister (who is 17) left home to live with some friends in a flat, because she couldn't take any more of it My parents' relationship got so bad that they split up and now the house is being sold. My father lives in a flat three miles away, and my mother doesn't know where she's going to live. All this happened in one year, and nobody wrote to tell me about it. Although I had the best year of my life, I wish I hadn't gone away. If I had been around I'm sure I could have helped and probably prevented all this happening. I feel so guilty and I am at my wits end to know how to help them now. Any suggestions?
Gareth, Glamorgan

A *Don't feel guilty. Your family are responsible for their own lives, and everything probably would have happened whether you were around or not. Just be thankful that they were considerate enough not to tell you what was going on. They did not want to spoil your year away, and I'm sure they are happy that you had such a good time. All you can do now is support each parent and your sister as best you can, and be careful not to take sides.*

Q My father used to be a real high flyer and we lived in a large house, had 2 cars, a boat, holidays abroad 3 times a year, in fact the best of everything. Then my father's business collapsed which meant he lost everything, and then my parents split up. I now live with my mother in a little flat, she goes out to work long hours because we've no money. There's no car, no luxuries, no holidays any more, and I had to leave my private school to go to a state school where I have nothing in common with the other boys.

I hate my life now, and my mother is always miserable too. I always used to look up to my father, but how can I forgive him for what he's done to us?
David, Gerrards X (13)

A *You must stop feeling sorry for yourself, and you really mustn't blame your father for what happened. Try to understand what a terrible blow it must have been for your father to have his business collapse (probably through no fault of his own), and to lose everything including his marriage. Both your parents are doing the best they can for you now, and you must try to help them by doing your best at school, and making an effort to get on with the other boys and be friends with them. Be thankful that you have been lucky enough to have experienced a life-style that most of them will never know. It is unfair to give your parents any more worries. Please try to make them proud of you.*

Q My Dad died last year and I really miss him. My Mum misses him a lot too, and when I go to bed I often hear her crying in her bedroom. I don't like to mention him much any more in case I upset her. How do we cope with all this?
Darren (10), Wimbledon

A *I think that it is very important for you and your mother to talk about your father. She is also probably afraid to mention him, in case she upsets you. Your father is still part of your lives and you must never forget him. If you could both have a good cry together and remember all the happy times you had with your father, it would help. Also suggest to your mother that you both go to talk to your local Cruse group, the organisation for the bereaved, and see if they can help. Call 0181 940 4818 for details.*

NEW BEGINNINGS

'But You're Not My Father!' Problems Between Step-Parents/New Partners and Children

Q My fiancee's children have coped well with the divorce, and they seem to have accepted my relationship with their mother. However, since I moved in with them, I naturally needed to play the role of parent more than before, and I can't seem to get any discipline. They are well behaved when my fiancee is about, but when she leaves me alone with the kids they start to play up. I ask them to stop being naughty and they just ignore me. If I lose my temper they just sneer 'you can't tell us what to do - you're not our father!' Sometimes when their Mum reappears they start crying and telling tales about me shouting at them. I think they are turning her against me - she never sees them being so naughty so she can't understand why I get so cross, and she seems to disbelieve me when I explain. I never foresaw this when we got engaged, and now I'm worried as to whether marrying a ready-made family will work. Can you help?

Edward, St Johns Wood

A *This is not an unusual difficulty. The children probably see you as interfering with the attention they used to get and resent your intrusion. Strangely the younger the children, the easier it is to cope with. The first thing to do is to stop feeling responsible for them; they are not your children and you do not have to control their behaviour. You do not have to be a disciplinarian - you can be their friend, and if you gain their confidence and respect as a friend you will be able to influence them a lot more than if you had just criticised and told them off! In so far as their naughtiness deteriorates into bad manners you can explain that bad manners do not make them attractive company, and then leave it to your fiancee to deal with. Until you are happy to be left alone with them, don't be.*

Q My father and mother got divorced, and my father married a woman who has two daughters. Since then he doesn't seem to care about me; I hardly ever see him, and my mother even had to remind him when it was my birthday (on the day). If I do speak to him he doesn't seem to be interested in anything I've done, and he just tells me all the 'wonderful' things my step-sisters have done which makes me feel terrible. Whatever I do or say it seems I can never be as good as his new family. How can I make him appreciate me?
Jo, Basildon

A *Because you see so little of each other you have grown apart, and you no longer seem, to your father, to be part of his life. Write him a letter saying how much you would like to see more of him, and how you would like to get to know him and his new family better. When you see him, show an interest in what they are all doing, and start to make friends with him and his family. If you become part of his life again, he will show interest in you. Whatever happens, you have a lovely mother who obviously cares deeply for you and really appreciates you, and it is important never to neglect her.*

Q My parents decided to get divorced and didn't tell me and my sister about it until we were having breakfast together one morning. They hadn't been getting on very well with each other for a few years, but I didn't realise how bad it was. They told us they were planning for one of them to move out, and in the end my father left and my sister and I landed up staying at home with my mother. My father has now told us that he is living with a girlfriend, that he wants to marry her and have more children, and that she's 20 years younger than him! I hate living at home with my mother and I hate my father for what he's doing to us, and I can't concentrate at school any more. My teachers just go on at me because my grades are getting lower, and I am sick of everyone and everything. Please help.
Kirsty, Plumstead

A If your parents were not getting on, they were right to get divorced to try to save you from living in an unhappy atmosphere. Now that he is no longer with your mother, you mustn't blame your father for accepting a chance to be happy with someone new. Your mother is doing her very best for you and your sister and she really deserves some help from you. Try to stop feeling sorry for yourself and be more considerate to those around you. Getting low grades at school is no way to get back at your parents - you are only being a fool to yourself and you will be the one who suffers. Your teachers realise this, and as they want to see you get the best you can out of life, they are naturally 'going on' at you. Don't forget that if you have problems you can always go to see your school counsellor.

Q My step-father wants to have sex with me. It started when I was 14 and he used to touch my bottom every time I was near him and make suggestive remarks. I told my mother, but she never believed me because he always came up with a 'perfect' excuse whenever she talked to him about me. When I was 15 he started coming into my bedroom to 'talk' to me. He told me that girls of my age needed practice with sex and that he could help me. I started locking my bedroom door and then one day when my mother was out, he sat beside me on the settee and started to touch me and kiss me. I screamed and pushed him away and ran out of the room. When my mother returned I told her everything that had happened, but after talking to my step-father she didn't believe me, and was angry with me for 'making up' stories about him - I wanted to commit suicide! They've now sent me away to boarding school to 'pull myself together' and I never want to go home again. I'm frightened of what my step-father might try to do with me, and I'm frightened of what I might do to him if he tries. My mother has been diagnosed as having a heart problem and so I can never tell anyone my secret in case I kill her with worry! I'm feeling desperate, please help me!
Rowena, High Wycombe

A You must talk to Matron at your boarding school as soon as possible, she is there to help you with any problems you may have. Tell everything that has happened to you, and also that you do not wish to go home - she will know what to do for you. Do you have any relatives or friends that she could arrange for you to stay with while the problem with your step-father is being sorted out? You can also call CHILDLINE at any time on 0800 1111 whenever you need to talk to someone or ask for help. Don't worry about your mother, you won't kill her, but she really needs to understand the truth about your situation as soon as possible, for all your sakes.

Q Mum and Dad don't live together any more, so my brother and I (I'm 9 and he's 7) live with Mum all week, and spend most weekends at Dad's place where he lives with his girlfriend who's called Pat. We really like seeing Dad but Pat is awful. When we arrive she makes us take our shoes off in case we muck up her carpets, and then she makes us have a bath (even if we tell her we've just had a bath). She won't let Dad and us stay in on Saturdays even if it's raining, because she has to clean the house. We can't play in the house, and we have to be quiet because she can't stand noise. Dad doesn't like to upset her and we have a miserable time. Mum says we have to go there, do you think we do?
Liam, Berks

A Surely Pat is doing you a favour by sending you out all day on Saturday, and letting you have your Dad to yourselves. Your Mum obviously thinks that it is important for you to see as much as you can of your father, and she probably needs some time to herself too. You know you will have a bath when you arrive at your Dad's house, so don't wash before you go! Try to save all your quiet pursuits, like reading and playing board games, for the weekend, or if you want to make a noise go and play outside if you can. Try to keep Pat's house rules and try to like her, and I am sure that as she gets to know you she will become less fussy. If your Dad likes her, she can't be too bad!

Q My parents split up when I was 8 and my mother has recently started dating a new boyfriend. She is very happy and likes him a lot. When I am on my own with him he hits and tells me how much I'm like my father, and says if I tell my mother he'll kill

me. I am now 10 and very scared. What should I do? I love my mother very much and I don't want him to be my step-father.
Joshua, Hartlepool

A There is no way that your mother's boyfriend should be allowed to hit you and threaten you. If you are afraid to tell your mother about what is happening, tell your father, a relative or teacher, as soon as possible and let them sort things out for you. It would be a good idea to ask your father if you can stay with him for a few days while all this is happening. Be brave, but tell someone now!

Q My father's got a new girlfriend, and whenever I go out with them both I have a good time because I really like her. He says I mustn't tell my mother about his girlfriend because she'll be upset. I don't like lying to her when she asks me what we did, and so I just don't say anything and I know she feels hurt. What should I do?
Alex, Chelmsford

A Tell your father what you are doing, and also how hurt your mother feels about it. Suggest that she might feel a lot less hurt if she were to be told the truth by both of you.

Q My father left us three years ago, and although he was not at all like me (he was very quiet and hardly said anything) I found it very difficult to cope with him not living with us any more. My mother eventually met someone else and they've just got married. She's happy with him, but I can't cope with living with this replacement 'father'. He has always tried to be friendly, but I just go quiet and don't talk to him. I know they are both upset about what's happened to me, but I just can't help myself and I can't wait to be 16 (I'm 14) so I can move out. What shall I do in the meantime?
Francke, Antwerp, Belgium

A *Maybe you* are *like your father because he went silent when he was unhappy at home, and you are doing the same. Give your mother a break and don't try to spoil the happiness she has found now. Don't think of your step-father as being a 'replacement' father, just try to get to know him and be friends with him. He is offering you friendship so be civil and offer some back; it is really not his fault that you resent him so much. Make the most of what you have; you are a lucky girl to be with two adults who obviously care so much about you and want to have you live with them. The thought of moving out may seem wonderful to you, but do be sensible about it. Where would you go and how would you support yourself? You would encounter many more problems than you have now. You do not mention whether you see your father on a regular basis - I feel that it is very important for you not to lose touch with him.*

'She Never Did That With Me!'
Problems Between 'Ex's'
and 'Ex's' New Partners

Q I've been divorced from my wife for a year, and although we had bitter times during the divorce settlement, we have become good friends. We are on such friendly terms that my ex-wife now tells me everything she gets up to, including all the intimate details of her sex life with her new boyfriend. I know I'm probably being stupid and over sensitive, but when she tells me what they get up to it really upsets me, because she never did any of that with me! Am I being unreasonable?
Paul, Newbury

A *You are not being unreasonable, and there is no reason why you should have to listen to such things. Maybe your wife doesn't realise that she is upsetting you, or maybe for reasons of her own, she is trying to make you jealous. In future refuse to listen, and ask her how she would feel if you told her about all the new and exciting intimate details of your sex-life!*

Q I got divorced two years ago, and my new partner Richard has been a widower for nearly 10 years. Although I know he cares for me, I find it very hard competing with a 'ghost'. He is constantly telling me what a wonderful person his wife was, and how perfect she was in every way. I know this to be totally untrue as his family has told me they had a lot of marital problems just before her death. Yet Richard puts her on such a pedestal, he makes me feel a real failure by comparison. I know I can never take her place, but must I always live in her shadow?
Andrea, Swindon

A *No you must not. Whenever a loved one dies we tend to forget the bad times and accentuate the good. I think you should explain to Richard how his comments about his wife are affecting you. Tell him that you have no wish to lessen his memory of her, but you are with him now not her, and you are an entirely different person. You would like him to start appreciating your good points and not dwell on the bad in comparison to her. You have no wish to replace his feelings for her, but if he can't live in the present then you can have no future together.*

Q I was married for 10 years to my wife and we had some good times together, but eventually we grew apart, and on a business trip I met and fell deeply in love with a divorced lady. My wife was devastated when I told her, and could not believe that I no longer wanted to be with her. I left home a year ago to live with my new partner, and although my wife and I are going through divorce proceedings, she just won't let go. She hounds me with phone calls day and night, pleading with me to go back to her. She writes letters to my partner telling her to give me up, and even came round to see her whilst I was at work last week. I do my best to support my wife as well as I can, but I am obviously finding it difficult supporting two homes. My wife thinks that I am concealing 'my fortunes' from her and that my partner is rich as well. She is making more and more demands on us, and although we are extremely happy together, we are finding the situation to be quite a strain on our relationship. I don't want to hurt my wife any more, but I really don't know what to do. Please advise me.
Anthony, Ascot

A *That's what happens when you walk out on one to set up*
home with another! There is no reason why your wife should be a
good loser - good losers are people who never expected to win in the first
place. This has obviously been a terrible blow to your wife's self esteem
and she is feeling very lonely and deserted, and she resents seeing someone
else having the fruits of your career development which she helped support.
You will have to declare your assets in an affidavit in the divorce
however, and indeed it would be folly to try to conceal any of them.
Your wife will then have to accept your financial position and let the
Courts decide what she is entitled to. As long as your wife thinks she is
putting a few 'spokes in the wheel' of your new relationship she will
continue to hassle you. If you both put on a united front and always
appear happy and relaxed, and are friendly and welcoming to your wife
if she phones or visits your home, she will eventually give up the fight
and hopefully accept the situation.

Q My ex-husband (James) lives with his new partner
(Lucy), and our children (aged 14 and 12) spend every other
weekend with them at their home. The children love being with
Lucy, who is a lot younger than me, and talk incessantly about her
and what they got up to with her, when they are home with me.
They seem to hang on her every word, and now whenever they
have problems they don't consult me, they phone Lucy! Sometimes
when I tell them not to do something they tell me it's alright because
Lucy says so, and sometimes when I ask why they don't wear certain
clothes any more they tell me that Lucy thinks the clothes are
unfashionable! I try to keep my cool but really all this is becoming
too much, and I am beginning to dislike Lucy intensely. What do I
do about it?
Penny, Bracknell

A *Be very firm with your children and tell them that while*
they are under your roof, they live by your rules and not Lucy's. If
they don't want to wear some of their clothes it is up to them, but you are
not going to buy them any new ones. Also they should ask your permission
before they use the telephone, and if you don't want them to phone Lucy
for advice, don't let them. Organise a babysitter one evening and arrange
to meet James and Lucy to discuss the children. Tell them what has been

going on and ask for their help - you might even find that when Lucy tells them not to do something, the children say it's alright because Mummy says so!

Q My boyfriend Mick left me when our baby girl was 7 months old. We were living on my salary until I went on maternity leave (Mick was an art student). Then he went to work for a while, but in the end he said he felt 'trapped' and needed to pursue his artistic career. Now he lives on the dole and gives us just a few pounds a week (even though I am sure he is earning some cash by selling his pictures), yet he expects frequent access to our baby. I am now working all hours, relying on my mother or sister to babysit, and I see no reason to disrupt our routines to accommodate Mick's erratic student timetable if he is not prepared to support his child. What are my rights?
Karen, Barking

A *If Mick has not got a court order entitling him to see his child, then you are doing nothing wrong at present by preventing him from seeing his daughter. It is likely that he could get such an order, and therefore it might be best to come to an agreement with Mick as to definite times when he can visit or take her out. If he has to cancel any of these arrangements and you cannot alter your commitments, then it is his hard luck. I also think that it is only fair on your daughter to allow her some time with her father, and she might resent you in later years if you do not.*

Q We recently got divorced and as my ex-husband's family live in Iran and he has also been offered a job out there, there's nothing to keep him in England now. Although we still are at 'loggerheads' he loves our two children (who live with me) very much, and I am terrified he is going to try to take them with him. How can I stop him?
Margaret, London

A *If you genuinely fear that your ex-husband may intend to abduct your children, you must contact your solicitor and the police at once so that they can take steps to stop him. If you have a residence order then no one can take the children abroad without the written consent of both parents or the court's permission. The only exception to this is that the parent with the residence order can take the children temporarily abroad on a holiday providing it is for less than a month. Do not delay in acting now because once the children have left the United Kingdom, the authorities here are very limited in what they can do to assist in getting them returned.*

Q My wife and I are going through divorce proceedings and she is now living with her boyfriend and our son (Andrew) aged 6. I have to talk to her on the phone quite often about the sale of our house, the divorce, what time I am collecting Andrew etc. and I feel very awkward when the new man answers the phone - I don't really know how to treat him. He manages to make himself scarce when I go round to collect Andrew, and so far we have only met briefly to be introduced and shake hands. How do I deal with this?

John, Stratford-upon-Avon

A *It sounds as if the boyfriend feels just as awkward as you, otherwise he would not make himself scarce when you collect Andrew. Why don't you break the ice by giving him a call and suggesting that you both meet for a drink and a chat. When you meet let him know how awkward you have been feeling, and also assure him in case he was worried, that you have no hard feelings towards him for living with Andrew and your wife. Hopefully you will both have a laugh, and it will certainly be better for Andrew if you can all meet and converse normally in future.*

Q My husband and I split up just over 4 months ago and I am now living with my boyfriend. Our best man at our wedding recently got engaged to my chief bridesmaid and they have asked me to their engagement party, and they have also invited my husband. When he heard that I was bringing my boyfriend to the party, my husband was furious and told our friends that he would not go if my boyfriend was there. They have now asked me not to bring my boyfriend as they really want my husband to come to the

party. I feel hurt that they have so little concern for me or my boyfriend's feelings. What shall I do?
Philippa, Birmingham

A I think in this instance you have to consider your friends' feelings before your own or your boyfriend's. It is a very awkward situation for them because both you and your husband are special friends of theirs, and they want you both to be at their engagement party. If your husband were to refuse to come, or if he did come with your boyfriend present and there was a bad atmosphere, both these scenarios would spoil their party. It is a special occasion for them, so do try to put them first - you can always leave early and meet your boyfriend later.

THE TWILIGHT
YEARS

'I Said Where's My Hat?
Not Feed The Cat!'
Problems experienced by Men

Q My wife and I are in our 70's and we are both hard of hearing. I now wear a hearing aid, but my wife refuses to admit to having a hearing problem and won't get one. Conversation between us is becoming so up-hill and difficult that I just give up. We live in a remote area of the country, and even when we have the chance to meet up with friends it's very awkward as my wife can't converse with them. I feel so lonely, what can I do?
Stan, Hexham

A None of us like to admit that we are growing old and developing all the usual physical problems that go with this. However I think you need to explain in no uncertain terms to your wife, by talking to her or writing it down, that in fact she has almost lost her hearing, and if she does not do something about it she is in danger of losing her friends. They will start to avoid her if it becomes such an effort to try and converse with her. Show her leaflets from the doctor on inconspicuous hearing aids, or if you can afford it, ask a private firm to send a consultant round to show her hearing aids that are so small, few people would even notice them. It is important that you enjoy the rest of your life, and if you can't make her understand the extent of the problem, ask your local GP to drop in for a chat with her. I'm sure you will find the doctor willing to do this, if only to prevent you becoming ill with depression.

Q All my working life I've been looking forward to my retirement. I've been looking forward to a time when my wife and I could do all the things we've never had time to do, and also to a time when we could be more sociable and invite our friends round or go out with them. This was to be a new life for us, a chance for us to start all over again and enjoy ourselves. The problem is that my wife doesn't seem to share my dream and all she wants to do is read the papers or watch the TV. She even seems ashamed of inviting friends round to our house. I feel cheated that I worked so hard, scrimped and saved, and missed out on so much in order for us to live life to the full when I retired, and now she's just not interested! What can I do?

Alfred, Biggin Hill

A *Although you have retired, your wife has not! In fact, having you around all the time probably means she is working harder than before, and she may not have the energy left to do anything other than read the papers or watch TV. She has also spent her married life being conditioned to a certain way of life, and maybe entertaining friends and enjoying herself is something that she is not used to. Unfortunately you, like many others, are now facing the end result of a lifetime's routine of not enjoying the present. Rome wasn't built in a day, and you can't change a lifetime's habit overnight; just take a deep breath, calm down and start to do things. Your wife is ashamed of your house, so why not move house? House hunting can be fun, and you could move away from the area that has created the habit and develop new habits. However, you have to be aware that moving house is extremely stressful and you may prefer to have alterations done to the house, and decorate it to her liking. Once the house is in order, your wife will probably want to invite friends round, and this in turn will produce reciprocal invitations from them. Your wife has been used to having her own space whilst you were working so hard, and so if you have always wanted to play golf for example, visit museums, or take up any other hobby or sport, go ahead and do it. Try planning weekend breaks or holidays with your wife that she would find hard to refuse. Whatever you do, start living in the present and enjoy every moment to the full.*

Q I'm 80 and my wife is in her late 60's. She wants us to move home while we are still able to do so, but we have such a wonderful home in such a glorious part of the countryside I couldn't bear to leave it. She wants to move to sheltered accommodation as soon as possible, as she fears that when we really need it we will not be able to find any. I do not want to go to sheltered accommodation as I would feel cooped up with other people around me. I love doing the gardening, and I love having space to do my own thing and go for walks down our country lanes. Although she is younger than me, my wife is less active and doesn't drive - she is now getting anxious about what will happen to us when I can no longer drive! We're not badly off and I would rather get occasional taxis if needs be, and would rather employ someone to help us in the house. I'm now getting panic attacks every time I think about the way she wants to change our life, and I'm becoming increasingly depressed. Please help.

Frank, Honiton

A It is extremely important that you take your courage in both hands, and explain very firmly to your wife what you are not willing to do. At the same time you need to take on board that she does have some valid points of view. Maybe while you are still able to drive, you could both look around at as many sheltered homes as possible and put your name down on waiting lists, simply as a precaution in case both or just one of you really need it in the future. If you can afford to employ them and have the room to house them, and you both could put up with the intrusion of having other people living in your house, a married couple would be ideal to help with the housekeeping and driving your wife around. You need to sort the problem out and compromise as soon as possible, otherwise you both may become seriously ill with worry and depression causing even worse problems. None of us know how many more years we have left to live, and it is of vital importance to appreciate and enjoy every precious moment you have.*

Q My wife is 85 and I am slightly younger. She's always had bags of energy and acted as if she were ten years younger. I have always found her zest for life very inspiring and attractive, however nowadays she worries me as she will not admit to herself that she is getting older, and I feel she takes far too many risks for her age. For example she still insists on climbing up ladders, even the one in the greenhouse! I love her very much and I'm so frightened she's going to kill herself. How do I get her to slow down and be more careful?

Basil, Brockenhurst

A Think yourself lucky that the only 'vegetable' you live with is the one that your wife likes to tend in the greenhouse! One way to avoid your wife having to take too many risks is to employ an odd-job man, or maybe you could hold the ladder while she climbs up and down it. Your wife has the right to live her life as she pleases, and if it pleases her to live her life dangerously, let her. It is better to have a shorter life full of excitement and pleasure, than a longer one which is less enjoyable and boring.

Q My wife has always been an easy going sort of person, but now she's getting on a bit (she's 71), she seems to be seems to be suffering from increased anxiety fears. For example she worries about what will happen to all our possessions when we die, and keeps sorting things out and putting things in order as if we're going to die next week! She is suffering from increased insomnia, and gets up in the middle of the night and just paces up and down the room. She suffers from claustrophobia in the home and will suddenly leave the table during a meal and go out for a walk. She refuses to go to the Doctor and says there is nothing a Doctor could do to help her. I'm at a loss to know what to do, and need your advice.
Reggie, Crawley

A I am sure that a Doctor could help your wife; she could possibly be suffering from agitated depression. If you can't persuade her to go to your local GP, maybe your children (if you have any), a close relative or friend could have a try. If nobody can persuade her to seek the Doctor's help, go and see him yourself, explain the situation and ask him to visit your wife - the sooner the better for both your sakes.

Q My wife has always kept the house in good order, but as she is getting older she is becoming unable to cope with things as well as she used to. Poor eyesight means the washing up (about which she used to be so meticulous) is no longer done thoroughly, and things are left greasy and soiled. A bad back means that corners she is unable to reach are left uncleaned, and cupboards are becoming filthy, but she no longer seems to notice. Any interference on my

part she regards as criticism as the household has always been her domain, and she refuses to get a cleaning lady or home help because she seems to feel threatened by the idea of such an intrusion on her privacy. I can't stand this drop in standards, what should I do?
Douglas, Telford

A I think you need to show a little more appreciation for what your wife does in the house. You also need to explain that your offers of help are not meant as a criticism, but that you genuinely want to do more in the home now for your own interest. Tell her that at your time of life you need to share more, and also to go out more and enjoy yourself with her. Suggest that you take it in turns to do the washing up, and occasionally when she goes out clean out a few cupboards and the corners that she can't reach (which you know she hasn't already noticed). Try to organise outings and activities with your wife so that she has less times for doing her household chores, and then eventually when she gets used to doing less, offer her the services of a cleaning lady. Tell her that no-one could ever do such a good job with the house as she has, but her company and her well-being mean more to you than a spotless tidy house!

Q A few years ago my wife renewed her acquaintance with a chap she nearly married when they were both in their early 20's. Last year he came to stay with us while he was on a business trip, and since then telephone calls between my wife and him have become increasingly frequent. My wife is quite open about their contact and admits that she is fond of him, and she tells me that his marriage is unhappy. He needs cheering up and she is his only life-line. She says he cannot tell his wife about her or that he stayed with us, as she gets insanely jealous! When I voiced my unease about their increasing closeness, my wife laughed it off and said she would never leave me. She is a youthful 58 and a very attractive woman, whilst I am twelve years her senior and had a heart attack last year. Though fully recovered I cannot rid myself of the idea that she is waiting for me to die so that they can be together. I dare not ask her to break contact with him as I fear that they would carry on behind my back, which would be even worse. I am quietly going out of my mind. Have you any suggestions?
Ben, Sunbury

A Talk to your wife's friend as soon as possible, and tell him he is getting too dependent on your wife and that you're not happy about it. Suggest that if he and his wife have marriage problems they should go together to a Marriage Guidance Counsellor for help - he can find Relate in his local telephone directory. Also suggest that he and his wife come to stay with you and your wife for a short break, so that you can develop a friendship between all four of you. Also please stop worrying and relax, because it is most likely that your wife is just innocently enjoying helping an old friend. Take her away on holiday, give her a good time and then explain exactly how you feel, and how much unhappiness this friendship is causing you at present. Be strong and I'm sure things will work out well for you. Good Luck.

Q My wife and I both have separate bank accounts and we are reasonably well off, but my wife gives all her money to our children and grandchildren and spends nothing on herself or me. She lives her life through her grandchildren and ignores me. In fact I don't think she'd notice if I just disappeared for a week. Should I?
Cyril, Frinton-on-Sea

A Your wife probably thinks you both have everything you want and need, and sees no need to spend money unnecessarily on either of you. She probably feels that her children and grandchildren have a greater need for the money, and it obviously gives her great pleasure in helping to enrich their lives - after all, it is her money in her own bank account to do with as she pleases. However that is no excuse for her to ignore you, and although you do not need her money you need her love and attention. Ask her away for a week's holiday, preferably somewhere remote where she has to give you her full attention, and set about wooing your wife back. If she refuses to go, well you have only got one life and so you might as well enjoy it - disappear away for a week on your own and see what life brings!

'I Don't Feel Needed Any More'
Problems experienced by Women

Q Both my children are married with families and live a long way away from me. I have been happily living alone in my flat since my husband died five years ago, but recently my balance started to go and for no reason at all I just fall down. When I go out I have to hold on to someone if I cross the road, in case I fall down in the middle of it. My family say they are worried about me and want to put me in an old people's home. My Doctor says I can't manage on my own and need help but I can't afford it. I would be happy living with either of my children but none of them want me, and I do *not* want to be disposed of into a home. I don't feel needed any more, and I really don't know where to turn to for help. Can you help me?
Eve, Brentford

A I suggest you make enquiries about sheltered accommodation, where you would have your own flat but there is always a warden on duty to check that all is well, and for sudden emergencies. You would have the companionship of other people of a similar age, but still retain your independence. Maybe you could ask your children to seek out such a place in their area so that you would be near enough for visits but you would not interfere with each other's day to day lives. Until then you need to ask your doctor to arrange for the maximum input of help that can be provided for you, such as home helps and meals on wheels. I also think that a special alarm which you would wear all the time, and which when pressed in an emergency rings selected telephone numbers to warn people that something is amiss, is essential for you. Please try not to think that your children don't want and need you, because they don't want you to live with them. Having a relative come to live with them can be very disruptive, and place great strains on any family for whatever reasons. They have their own reasons for deciding that the situation would not work, and I think you must accept them with good grace and get on with your life.

Q my husband has always been a very active man and used to play hard as well as working hard. He recently retired and his character seems to have changed. He doesn't know what to do with himself anymore and is under my feet all the time. I have been used to space and privacy all these years while he's been a workaholic, and I just can't adjust to this change of situation. I am getting more and more irritable with him and resent his intrusion into my life. Please help.
Edith, Taunton

A Your husband most likely feels completely lost, useless, frustrated and depressed with his dramatic change of circumstance. I advise you to urge your husband to go to visit his local GP as soon as possible, to make sure that he is not suffering from clinical depression. It is bound to take him a while to adapt to his new situation, and he needs all the support and encouragement you can give him. Encourage him to develop new hobbies and interests; it may not happen overnight, but eventually he will find his feet and you will gain some space. You need to compromise as well, and this will mean doing things together more than you used to. If you find this difficult, go together for some counselling to look for compromises. Think of your husband's retirement as a new challenging phase in your life, rather than as a nuisance.

Q We have been married for forty years and I have always done everything in the house without help from anyone. I have done the cooking, the cleaning, the shopping, the gardening, the decorating, brought up three children, nursed the family when they were ill, and I have not begrudged them one minute of it. However, I really thought that when my husband retired from work and had more time on his hands he would help me. I thought he would share the household tasks and make life a little easier for me. He does nothing! He just sits around and expects me to wait on him hand and foot like the slave I have always been to him! My resentment is destroying our relationship, and I am beginning to dislike my husband. What should I do?
Iris, Finchley

A You must say something to your husband. You must sit him down and tell him how you feel in a calm non-threatening manner, and not in an aggressive or resentful way. If you have 'waited on him hand and foot' all your married life without complaint, he has naturally got used to this way of life. Also don't forget that maybe when you got married this was the accepted role of a wife and mother. He probably has no idea that you want him to help; give him a chance and just ask. As well as asking for his help, you could also put in a request for a cleaner!

Q My husband is 75 and has started flirting with young girls. It doesn't matter where he is - in a shop, on the bus, on the beach - he has to stop and chat them up. In general they tolerate him and invariably smile, but sometimes I can see their eyes glazing over and I squirm with embarrassment. He's becoming a dirty old man and doesn't understand what a fool he's making of himself. What can I do?

Peggy, Porthcawl

A The problem is that although we all grow older physically, inside we very often still feel like a teenager! Try changing your way of thinking, and understand how difficult it is for your husband to accept old age. Try looking on with amusement and pride that there is 'life in the old dog yet'! If you get very embarrassed just walk away, after all it is not you that is being made to look a 'fool'. Also try to interest him in new hobbies and activities that he can do alone or together with you, and hopefully these will take his mind off chatting-up young girls.

Q My husband and I are both in our 70's and he's suddenly getting more amorous towards me! I still love him but I find the idea of sex at our age rather unpleasant. I thought we had finished with that side of our marriage at least ten years ago. How should I deal with this situation?

Ruby, Golders Green

A Many women have the opposite problem with their husband, and would be envious of you! Be pleased that your husband is still sexually interested in you, and go to your doctor to see if taking hormone tablets might make you sexually interested in him. Of course there are many things you can do to pleasure your husband, even if you don't want him to pleasure you. I would suggest that you do this often enough to keep him happy, but not so often that it will make you unhappy.

Q My husband died a few years ago and I still miss him very much. We were always very close and neither of us had much time for making other friends, we just loved being together. I am now 69 and want to go out and meet other people, but I find that whatever I join or activity I undertake, I only seem to meet old ladies with whom I do not seem to have a lot in common. Where are all the men of my age, surely they can't all have passed away?
Esme, Melton Mowbray

A Sadly I think you will find that statistics show there are less men than ladies of your age group. You could try taking up male dominated activities, or if you can afford it, take yourself off on a cruise. You could always start your own activities group and advertise for men to join it! My advice to you though is to stop looking for a man, and start enjoying the life you lead at present. You have been used to just being in male company, and there are probably many other ladies in a similar circumstance to your own with whom you would have a lot in common. Concentrate your efforts at present on finding such a lady; you will find life a lot more fun if you have a friend to share experiences with.

Q My husband is 67 and he retired two years ago. I have a part-time job in reception at the local medical centre. I enjoy my work and my colleagues are very nice. My husband has recently become very moody and admitted he was upset when I made a frivolous comment to friends of ours about the fact that I am now the bread winner. I am glad to be able to 'do my bit' after all the years during which he worked so hard and was the chief earner, but he resents me being out in the world and mixing with people while he is stuck at home. I have offered to give up my job if it hurts his pride, but he admits that we need the money. How can I repair his wounded pride? I could retire in 5 months when I am 60, but would be happy to keep my job for at least another five years. I don't know what to do.

Dorothy, Sheerness

A It is not a question of what you should do, more a need for your husband to get off his backside and go out and do something! If he does not want to, or is unable to work, then suggest that he interests himself in new hobbies or activities, or even helps with voluntary schemes - in this way he will also be out in the world of meeting people. It is unfair of him to envy your freedom and enterprise, and in so doing try to bring you down. Be proud of what you are achieving for the good of you both, and try to ignore your husband's uncharitable attitude!

Q I am 15 years younger than my husband, and throughout our marriage he has always been the 'boss' and I have always been the 'little lady'. Now that he is in his late 80's he is finding it increasingly difficult to cope with our affairs, but he still won't let me help him or share information about any money difficulties we may have. He gets so confused and I am sure everything is in such a muddle. How can I help sort things out without offending him?

Alice, Ewell

A Sit down and talk to him. Tell him how much you have always appreciated the way he has looked after you and sheltered you from financial matters. Explain that everyone gets themselves into muddle sometimes, and that now you would like to help him sort out his 'temporary' muddle. Then if he lets you share the responsibilities you will hopefully gain his confidence, and he might eventually let you take over. You could also enlist the help of your solicitor or accountant to talk to him, and to help him sort out his affairs. They are of course bound by professional confidence not to disclose any information to you. If at a later date your husband gets into such a bad state of confusion that he can't manage any of his affairs, his doctor will certify him incapable of managing his affairs and therefore financially vulnerable. The Protection Division of the Courts could then appoint a Receiver to take over his affairs.

'You'll Miss Me When I'm Gone'
Problems Between Elderly Parents
and their Children

Q I lead a very busy life as a single mother trying to cope with running my own business, looking after two children and running the home. My mother used to live 20 miles from us and although I tried my best to visit as much as I could (and although she had lots of friends, I know how much she looked forward to our visits) something 'more important' used to crop up at the last minute to prevent us from going to see her. We often had to disappoint her, and one day she said 'You'll miss me when I'm gone'. Well she died in her 80's last week whilst I was on a business trip, and I can never forgive myself for neglecting her so badly, and I really miss her. I feel so guilty I can't concentrate on anything, and I know my children are upset that I cry so much. How can I come to terms with my guilt?
Stella, Windsor

A *Everyone feels guilty when a loved one dies. We all wish that we had said or done certain things, we also suffer regrets about what we did do, and there is a sense of desperation inside us as we realise that it is just too late to do anything about it. However none of us is perfect, and I'm sure that your mother understood how difficult your life was to organise. You must have made her very happy when you did visit her, in order for her to miss seeing you and her grandchildren so much. We all have to make our own happiness (we can't live our lives through our children), and I'm sure that your mother had a happy fulfilled life if she had so many friends around her. Death is never convenient, and even if you had not been away on a business trip you could not have guaranteed being with her when she died. Remember with your children all the happy times you had with their grandma, and if you can, try not to cry so much in front of the children if it upsets them. However although time is a great healer you need to let yourself grieve, and the more tears you shed now, the quicker you will be able to come to terms with your loss. Talking to someone might also help, and if you phone CRUSE, the organisation for the bereaved, they will be happy to do so. Their helpline telephone number is 0181 332 7227.*

Q I have two wonderful grandchildren, Stephen (6) and Jenny (4), whom I love very much and I know they love me too. The problem is that I don't see very much of them as my daughter says I spoil them, and she tries to keep them away from me as much as possible. I know she finds it difficult bringing up the children on her own as well as having to do a full time job since her husband walked out, and I would be only too willing to help her out with baby-sitting, but she won't hear of it. I don't mean to spoil the children, but I suppose I do buy them presents and give them treats such as sweets when I see them, because I want to do as much as I can for them in the short space of time I am allowed to be with them. I love my daughter and want to do the best for her and the children. What do you think I should do?
Doreen, Ipswich

A *Try to find a time when the children are not around, to have a chat with your daughter on your own. Tell her that you have no wish to undermine her authority with her children, and you are very sorry if that is the way it has seemed to be. Ask her how she would like you to behave with them, and when or whether you would be able to give them some treats, and if so what treats she would like those to be. Tell her how proud you are of her and the way she is bringing up her children, as well as coping with a full time job. Offer your services and wait for her to ask you for help - I suspect that won't be a long wait!*

Q My mother keeps knitting me jumpers. Now that she finds it hard to get out and about, she says she likes to feel she is doing something useful. The results are usually shapeless and unfashionable and not the sort of thing I would wear, but I say I like them to be polite and because I don't want to hurt her feelings. Most of them end up being taken to the charity shop unworn. It hurts me to do this, and it breaks my heart that she spends so much of her limited money on wool and wastes so much effort. I don't want to destroy her raison d'être, so what can I do?
Melissa, Penge

A *Try not to think of your mother's knitting as a useless waste of effort, but as a fulfilling pastime that gives her great pleasure, and make sure you always wear one of these jumpers whenever you visit her. If you are worried about her spending her limited money on wool, why not donate the wool yourself and tell her that your friends have admired your jumpers so much they would like her to knit for them. The jumpers can still go to the charity shop, where I'm sure they will end up keeping someone warm and happy!*

Q My husband and I are retired, and my son-in-law's business is in financial difficulties. If my husband and I sell our house and move to somewhere smaller, we could raise enough capital to help them out of their current difficulties. My daughter says they don't need our help and must solve their own problems. My husband tends to agree with her, but they have two children to bring up and half their lives still ahead of them, and we would be just as happy somewhere smaller. I don't feel right living in such comfort in a beautiful big house, while they are struggling so hard. It would give me such joy to be able to help out in this way. How can I persuade my husband?
Janet, Edenbridge

A *Your husband and your daughter are absolutely right. Everyone has the right to be allowed to make their own mistakes and then sort out the problems. They will be wiser for the experience and better equipped to cope with future difficulties should they ever arise.*

Your daughter and son-in-law have their pride, and their embarrassment in accepting your help could lead to resentment should you make such a sacrifice for them. When they feel they need your help they will ask for it, and until then do not try to persuade your husband to sell your house - please sit back and enjoy the fruits of both your labours.

Q My mother always watches 'Crime Watch' and seems to believe everything she reads in the papers or sees on television. As a result she perceives the world as a dangerous and threatening place. She is afraid to go out in case either her house is burgled or she is mugged in the street, even though she lives in a small country town. She worries about me living in London although I am 48 years old, and is always anxious about the amount of driving I do for my work. She thinks I'll be murdered at the roadside if my car breaks down! How can I convince her that most people are nice and considerate, and that the world is not the evil place she sees it to be?
Marilyn, London

A *It seems to me that you need to gain some of your mother's pessimism, and she needs to gain some of your optimism for a better balanced view on life. It is good to try to see the best in people until you are proved wrong, but there are occasions when a little caution is apt. I advise you to invest in a mobile phone to have with you in the car in case you break down. Also contact your mother's local police station who will have an advisory service for personal security and also security of the home. Hopefully these measures will help put your mother's mind at rest.*

Q All our friends have grandchildren, but neither one of our children seems to show any interest in settling down and raising a family. Our son is nearly 40, our daughter is 35 and both of them are just happy thinking about their careers, new cars and where they are going to enjoy their next holiday. I feel that they live very selfish lives, and I am also upset that we are to be denied grandchildren. Is it all our fault, and if so where did we go wrong?
Arthur, Market Harborough

A I really do not think you went wrong at all. You must
have done everything right to bring up two happy, independent
and obviously capable adults. There is no rule that says your children
should produce offspring, and please don't make them feel guilty if they
decide not to. Also your own personal happiness should not be dependent
on living life through possible grandchildren. We all have to make our
own happiness, and you and your wife can lead happy and fulfilled lives
through enjoying hobbies, studies, travel and of course your own children.
It is not a necessity to have grandchildren to enjoy life!

Q I retired five years ago, and life is not so easy financially
for my wife and I as it used to be. We have one daughter of 25,
whom we had late in life. She is a student and unmarried mother,
and we have supported her up till now. The problem is that I don't
know how longer I can go on doing this, because I have borrowed
money already against our assets and I only receive a small pension.
My daughter has never earnt any money in her life, and we are so
worried for her and our grandchild. How can we tell her how badly
off we are at present?
Harry, Crewe

A I think that it is not a question of how *you tell your*
daughter about your financial problems, but *when. Your daughter*
has been very fortunate up till now to have such kind and loving parents
to support her financially, and I am sure emotionally, through college
and motherhood. However there comes a time when we all have to accept
responsibility for our lives and actions, and I think that this is your
daughter's time. I am sure that your daughter would not want you both
to suffer hardship for her sake, and of course it helps no-one if you make
yourselves ill with worry - that can only add to her burden. You can still
give her valuable help with looking after her child and baby-sitting, to
enable her to work or study. Also she will be able to sign on at her local
social security office for financial help. So long as you are always there
with emotional and practical support, she will be fine.

Q I am a widow in my eighties, and I have two daughters and four grandchildren. I know that I have not many years left to live and I am beginning to worry about my will. I know that both my daughters have always admired my husband's oil painting collection (all the paintings are of a similar size and value) and in particular there is one painting which both of them covet. I cannot divide the painting in two and I know one of them must be disappointed when I'm gone, and I am so afraid that this will cause a rift between them. I would like to sort the matter before I die, so that I can help with any problems brought about by my decision. However I cannot decide who should have the painting, or how to broach the subject with them, so what shall I do?
Florence, Brighton

A *I think that you should call a meeting with your daughters and explain your concerns. As all the paintings are of a similar size and value there are two choices: either the painting is to be sold and the money divided between the two of them, or they could share the painting by each having it for a period of 6 months at a time and interchanging it with one of the other paintings. Then whichever daughter survives the other, will inherit the painting. Put these two choices to your daughters, and then let them make the decision for you.*

Hillie Marshall's Agony Aunt page
on the INTERNET can be located
at the following address:

http://www.itl.net/goto/hotgossip

If you would like to contact Hillie directly,
please send e-mail to the following address:

hillie@camelotintl.com

By the same author:

Hillie Marshall's Guide To Successful Relationships

FOREWORD BY
Nicholas Parsons

SUMMERSDALE

"Indispensable". **Frank Skinner.**
"She's a natural." **The Independent**
Hillie Marshall's Guide To Successful Relationships is available through all good bookshops.
ISBN 1 873475 33 0   £6.99   Paperback